THE
OF UNSOLVED MYSTERIES

Did alien spaceships create the corn circles?
Was Napoleon murdered?
Do we have several past lives?

Prepare to be amazed, fascinated and perplexed by this
collection of intriguing real-life mysteries – from vanish-
ing people and uncanny psychic happenings to unsolved
murders, peculiar unidentified creatures, and historical
enigmas that have baffled us for centuries. Were the
young princes in the tower murdered by Richard III? Is
there a scientific explanation for UFOs? And human
levitation – is it possible? Not only will you find these
fifty extraordinary tales absorbing reading, you may
even have some ideas of your own. What do you think?
Can you fathom the truth behind any of these unsolved
mysteries?

Early Times is an independent newspaper for young
people which was launched in January 1988. With an
estimated readership of 200,000, the paper has attracted
much press coverage, particularly for its press-gang inter-
views of well-known politicians and personalities.

THE
EARLY  TIMES

The independent newspaper for young people

BOOK OF UNSOLVED
MYSTERIES

Illustrated by Keith Brumpton

PUFFIN BOOKS

PUFFIN BOOKS

Published by the Penguin Group

Penguin Books Ltd, 27 Wrights Lane, London W8 5TZ, England

Penguin Books USA Inc., 375 Hudson Street, New York, New York 10014, USA

Penguin Books Australia Ltd, Ringwood, Victoria, Australia

Penguin Books Canada Ltd, 10 Alcorn Avenue, Toronto, Ontario, Canada M4V 3B2

Penguin Books (NZ) Ltd, 182–190 Wairau Road, Auckland 10, New Zealand

Penguin Books Ltd, Registered Offices: Harmondsworth, Middlesex, England

First published 1993

1 3 5 7 9 10 8 6 4 2

Text copyright © Complete Editions, 1993

Illustrations copyright © Keith Brumpton, 1993

All rights reserved

Early Times would like to thank Hester Davenport for researching,
compiling and writing this book.

Typeset by Datix International Limited, Bungay, Suffolk

Filmset in 12/14 Monophoto Sabon

Printed in England by Clays Ltd, St Ives plc

Contents

First Things First

Here are fifty mysteries, from the classic story of the empty ship, the *Mary Celeste*, to UFOs, the great mystery of our own times. The order in which they are printed is completely random.

The idea for this book came from the former Managing Editor of *Early Times*, Alison Haymonds, who has given me a great deal of help and encouragement. I'd like to thank her, and members of my family and friends who've talked things over with me, made suggestions, lent me books, and sent me information.

Thanks also to my daughter Olivia, for being first reader of most of the mysteries. Her enthusiasm was another great encouragement.

I should like to dedicate this book to the memory of my father.

Hester Davenport

1

The *Mary Celeste*

In the middle of the Atlantic Ocean, on 4 December 1872, Captain Morehouse of the sailing-ship *Dei Gratia* spotted a similar two-masted trading vessel. His eye was caught by her erratic movements. As they drew near to each other Captain Morehouse hailed the strange ship, but without reply. There was no one on deck, no one at the wheel. The ship was being driven onward by her sails, though the top rigging flew in tatters.

At some stage the captain must have seen the ship's name – the *Mary Celeste*.

Captain Morehouse sent two seamen across in his

ship's boat to investigate, perhaps expecting to find a fever-ridden crew below. But there was no one on board.

On her unmanned journey she had shipped water in stormy seas, but not enough to be at risk of sinking. She carried plenty of food and drinking water and her cargo of barrels of alcohol was intact. Washing still hung on a line in the crew's quarters, and their pipes and tobacco lay there too. In the captain's cabin a log slate recorded a date, 25 November, and a last known position.

No ship's boat could be found, so it seemed that some ten days earlier, and five hundred miles away, the crew of the *Mary Celeste* must have abandoned their perfectly seaworthy ship.

The *Mary Celeste* and her cargo were valuable, so Captain Morehouse decided to split his own crew and sail both ships to Europe in order to claim salvage. Had he known the trouble this would cause him he would probably have left the ship to continue her lonely voyage.

The two ships reached Gibraltar, but there Captain Morehouse came up against a highly suspicious investigating officer who, though unable to prove it, clearly thought that the *Dei Gratia* was involved in some criminal activity. Captain Morehouse was eventually awarded only a fraction of the salvage money he might have expected.

What had happened on board the *Mary Celeste*? There have been plenty of colourful theories. Perhaps the ship was hit by a waterspout? If so, it hadn't done much damage. Or maybe a sea serpent picked the members of the crew off, one at a time – this would explain an apparent axe-mark on one of the ship's rails, perhaps made by a valiant seaman trying to fight the monster off before himself falling victim!

According to another idea the captain went mad,

jumped overboard, the crew dived or fell in too and all were gobbled up by sharks.

It's important to remember that no disorder was found on board, so explanations of piracy or mutiny won't do. Perhaps the crew were tempted by the alcohol and all got drunk and did something silly? But this was commercial alcohol, and quite undrinkable.

Was there, as suspected, a conspiracy between the two captains? Perhaps the men from the *Mary Celeste* were secretly set ashore with a promise that the salvage money would be shared. However, Captain Briggs of the *Mary Celeste* was known as a religious and moral man. His wife and two-year-old daughter were with him on this voyage, but he'd left his young son behind in America. That doesn't sound like the action of someone planning a new life.

So we are left to conclude that Captain Briggs did suddenly give the order to abandon ship. Possibly he believed that the cargo was about to explode – in moving into warmer waters the barrels might have begun to make strange hissing noises as they adjusted to the new temperatures. It's hard to believe that an experienced captain would panic so easily, but there is one further clue to support this theory.

A broken halyard (rigging rope) had to be repaired before the *Mary Celeste* could sail again. Perhaps, fearing calamity for whatever reason, Captain Briggs hurried his family and crew into the ship's boat, attaching it to the ship for easy return if nothing happened. Then in a sudden squall the rope snapped, and the *Mary Celeste* sailed on, leaving the captain to curse his stupidity.

There are a lot of maybes and mights about this theory, but making guesses is all we can do now to solve the riddle of the empty ship.

The *Mary Celeste* came to a sticky end too. For some years afterwards she continued as a trading vessel, until in 1885 she foundered on a reef off the coast of Haiti. It was strongly suspected that she'd been deliberately run aground.

She was then dowsed in kerosene and set on fire, thus ending her days in a blaze of flame.

Postscript: This ship is sometimes mistakenly called the *Marie Celeste*.

2

Crop Circles

What makes them? Flying saucers? Whirlwinds? Frantic hedgehogs? Ravenous rooks? Mad mushrooms? Or men with garden rollers?

The patterned circles which appear in the summer cornfields, mainly in southern England, first attracted attention in the early 1980s. These circles were just that – swirled circles in the corn, usually appearing overnight and ranging in diameter from less than one metre to over sixty.

Observers were impressed by the precision of the circular shapes and the regular, layered patterning of the corn within them. Corn damages easily, but there seemed to be no obvious sign of human or animal approach to the crops.

In these simple circles, the crop is swirled in a clockwise or anti-clockwise direction, or radiates out from the centre as spokes do in a wheel, but the flattened stalks are unbroken.

At the outer edges the flattening ends abruptly and the corn grows straight and tall again. Sometimes there is an outer ring in which the crop may be swirled in the opposite direction.

As the 1980s went on and media interest grew, the circle systems, at any rate those making the headlines, got more complicated. They began to appear in groups, evenly spaced like dots on a dice.

They were joined by lines to look like pairs of dumb-bells, or they sprouted spurs and were said to look like a

13

kind of writing. Was some unearthly intelligence using our cornfields to send us messages? Excitement grew, world-wide.

In the summer of 1991 ever more extraordinary geometric shapes were produced, along with 'insectograms' with antennae, 'whales', and even a wiggly shape known as 'the brain'.

Then came the dramatic revelation in *Today* newspaper: old-age pensioners from Southampton, Doug Bower and Dave Chorley, announced that they had been creating the shapes. They planned them at home, then set off at night, carrying tape recorders so that if challenged they could say they were making wildlife recordings. To reach the centre of the fields they used the tractor 'tramlines' and left no obvious pathways through the corn.

Nevertheless, corn circle fever continued. In 1992 yet more complicated shapes appeared; but also more hoaxers owned up, and a newspaper competition for circle-makers demonstrated that pattern-making in a cornfield at night is not all that difficult.

Sadly then it seems that we have to assume that all the bizarre shapes are the work of Doug and Dave or their kind. But many still feel that at least the simple circles, away from the tramlines, are genuine and connected neither with humans, nor aliens, nor hungry birds, nor mating hedgehogs, nor underground fungi.

After all, records of circles go back to times before the media gave them publicity. Indeed it is believed that stories in the seventeenth century of 'mowing devils' at work refer to crop circles.

Furthermore, there have been daytime witnesses of circle formation. Observers have seen dust flying up from where a circle was later found, and a peculiar humming noise has been heard as well. There are also reports of weird balls of light moving downwards at night, and though these sightings seem to support the alien spaceship theory, there is another explanation.

Terence Meaden, a meteorologist, has put forward the idea that the circles are created by localized whirlwinds.

He argues that the rolling hills of southern England allow the right climatic conditions for turbulent air movements to occur. A swirling eddy of air, which he calls a 'vortex', begins to spin – rather as waterspouts and dust devils do. It is probably electrically charged, thus explaining the sounds and lights.

The spinning air forms into a kind of doughnut shape, then sweeps downwards and outwards to form the circle.

In support of Meaden's theory a Japanese professor has reproduced mini-whirlwinds of this kind in his laboratory, forming small-scale circles in plates of aluminium powder.

Not everyone is convinced by Meaden's arguments, certainly not those who still want to believe that aliens are bouncing up and down in the cornfields, nor the hard-headed who think that Doug and Dave's revelations have put paid to the fuss about crop circles for good.

What will happen now? The media have lost interest and people are disillusioned. Will there be circles in our corn again? Summer wouldn't be the same without them.

3

The Princes in the Tower

Don't worry, boys, Richard'll fix it!

Black-hearted villain or noble hero? No English monarch has attracted such opposing views as King Richard III, who ruled from 1483–5. In Shakespeare's play about him he is cursed as a 'poisonous bunch-backed toad', but when he actually died the citizens of York mourned 'our good King Richard'.

Central to the issue is the question: did he order the killing of his nephews, the princes in the Tower?

King Edward IV, who died in April 1483, appointed his brother Richard as Lord Protector of the Realm while his son, Edward V, was growing up. Four weeks later Richard, then Duke of Gloucester, made a ceremonial entry into London with the new king. The twelve-year-old Edward, golden-haired and wearing a blue velvet riding-gown, contrasted with his dark uncle, dressed all in black.

Also riding with them was another young nobleman in black, Harry, Duke of Buckingham.

Edward was lodged in the Royal Apartments of the Tower of London. There he was joined by his younger brother, another Richard, Duke of York. The two boys were seen in the gardens playing and shooting with their bows and arrows.

Plans were made for Edward's coronation in June, but shortly beforehand the Duke of Gloucester announced that Edward IV had not been properly married to his queen so that he, Richard, was the true heir and king. Whether people believed him or not, the reign of Richard III began.

The two boys were moved from the Royal Apartments, though for a while they were still glimpsed at windows in the Tower. Then they vanished altogether from public sight.

Without any absolute proof it has always been assumed that at some stage they were murdered, and Richard has been suspected of giving the order for their deaths. Though the boys themselves could not have threatened his kingship, others might have rebelled in their names.

Against belief in Richard's guilt is knowledge of his long years of loyalty to Edward IV — Richard's motto was 'Loyalty binds me'.

The Duke of Buckingham, a man with royal ambitions of his own, has also been suspected. But although he might have been in the know it would not really have been possible for him to take action without Richard's authority.

We are left with a third suspect: Henry Tudor, who defeated Richard at the Battle of Bosworth to become Henry VII.

Had Richard secretly been keeping the boys alive somewhere their existence would certainly have been unwelcome to Henry, and he was ruthless enough to have disposed of them. It is odd that when Henry was listing all Richard's 'crimes' to justify his own taking of the crown he didn't include the brutal murder of two children.

But if the boys did survive Richard III, where had they been? There would have been servants to attend them, and to whisper their whereabouts.

Because the Tudors were anxious to blacken Richard's name it is difficult to sort fact from fiction after 1485. But one writer produced a history of Richard III by questioning men who lived then. Sir Thomas More's account contains mistakes, but there are reasons for thinking that he may have discovered the truth about the princes.

More says that before execution for treason in 1502 Sir James Tyrell confessed to having organized the princes' killing – on Richard's orders. One night he took two burly villains with him to the Tower, around the hour of midnight. They crept up to the boys' beds and 'suddenly lapped them up among the bedclothes', suffocating them. The bodies were then buried at the foot of a staircase under a pile of rubble.

What helps make this story believable is that in 1674, during the reign of Charles II, workmen digging under a Tower staircase found a box containing the skeletons of two children. Of course, the bones didn't come neatly labelled, but Charles felt sure they belonged to the princes and had them placed in a specially-designed urn in Westminster Abbey.

In 1933 this urn was reopened and the bones examined by medical experts, who identified them as belonging to boys aged about twelve and ten – Edward and Richard's ages in 1483. These findings are disputed by Richard supporters, however.

Despite the lack of final proof most historians think that Richard did have his nephews murdered in order to safeguard his seizure of the crown.

Was it, if so, a sudden yielding to temptation, or was he already coldly calculating his actions when he presented Edward to the cheering crowds? When a year later his own young son fell sick and died, did Richard have any sense that he had been justly punished?

4

The Versailles Ghosts

Time-travelling into the past happens often enough in books and films, but can it in reality? There is one intriguing story which, if you accept it, suggests that occasionally it can.

On 10 August 1901 two highly respectable ladies visited the magnificent Palace of Versailles near Paris, built by Louis XIV. Miss Annie Moberly, then aged fifty-five, was Principal of St Hugh's College for Women in Oxford; thirty-eight-year-old Miss Eleanor Jourdain was her new vice-principal.

After the main palace they set off to visit the Petit Trianon, the favourite retreat from court life of the ill-fated Queen Marie Antoinette, wife of Louis XVI. In

Excuse me, but d'you have the time?

1789

1789 during the French Revolution she had had to flee from mobs attacking Versailles; later her husband was guillotined and her son taken from her, before she herself was tried and executed.

For the two middle-aged ladies the afternoon was pleasant, with a refreshing breeze. They followed a path which led, they thought, to the Petit Trianon, but chatting together they lost their way and found themselves following a route which they could never afterwards retrace.

The day stopped seeming so pleasant; the breeze had disappeared and the atmosphere was oppressive. Miss Moberly wrote that everything suddenly looked unnatural and even the trees 'seemed to have become flat and lifeless, like a wood in a tapestry'. Feeling uneasy and depressed they walked on, and began to meet figures who later they felt convinced belonged to another age.

First there were two official-looking men, dressed in green uniforms and wearing queer little three-cornered hats. They answered the women's questions in a strange mechanical way.

On the steps of a small circular building was a dark, pock-marked man in a broad-brimmed hat and black cloak, whose expression they found evil and menacing.

They heard running steps but could see nobody till, out of thin air it seemed, a young man also in large hat and cloak and wearing buckled shoes, stood beside them telling them excitedly to 'cherchez la maison' (seek the house).

Following his directions they crossed a bridge over a small ravine and finally got to the back of the Petit Trianon. As they drew near the building Miss Moberly saw, though Miss Jourdain did not, a woman seated sketching. This figure turned and gazed straight at her.

Afterwards Miss Moberly came to believe that she had seen Marie Antoinette herself. Although when she first looked at portraits of the Queen she didn't recognize the face, she later came across a less flattering picture, and was convinced. She also recognized, from fashion plates by the Queen's dressmaker, the style of dress her sketching lady had been wearing.

After the meeting with 'Marie Antoinette' the two ladies went round to the front of the building and there found themselves clearly in the modern world again.

Perhaps because they didn't know each other well, it was a week before they discussed their strange experiences. But then they decided to write separate accounts of what they had seen and to research into the period.

What they learnt strengthened their belief that they had glimpsed the past: for example, they were excited when an old map was discovered which showed the little ravine they'd crossed, but couldn't find in the modern gardens.

They explained what they called 'an adventure' by suggesting that while she was in prison Marie Antoinette recalled her last days at Versailles so vividly that she left an imprint of her memory there, which the women picked up. (The pock-marked man was, they thought, a nobleman who helped bring about her destruction, the running man someone who tried to save her.)

It has been claimed, however, that what they really saw was a group of people in fancy dress. Moreover, despite some convincing detail, we need to be wary of accepting it all at face value.

No one has ever thought that the two ladies deliberately made anything up, but how reliable were their memories? A first rule if you have a ghostly experience is to write it down at once, without discussing it. But Miss Moberly and Miss Jourdain talked it over, perhaps influencing each other, and didn't write individual accounts for another three months.

Worse still, the versions which they eventually published were written even later, yet these add details, like the old-fashioned buckled shoes, which weren't in the first accounts. Could their memories really have improved with time?

So there have to be doubts about the 'adventure'. But it's also not to be doubted that most people would *like* to believe in it.

5

The Loch Ness Monster

Loch Ness, thirty-five kilometres long, 300 metres deep and one and a half kilometres across, is the largest stretch of fresh water in the British Isles. Hemmed in by mountains, its waters cold and inky black (because of all the peat dissolved in them), it looks just the place for a monster's lair. But has a mysterious beast ever lurked in its depths?

Although a few tales of water beasts date from early times, monster-spotting really got going after 1933. A report in the *Inverness Chronicle* claimed that a couple called Mackay had seen a huge creature, as big as a whale, plunging about in the loch. Later it turned out that this was something of an exaggeration – what Mrs Mackay said she'd really seen was a commotion in the water which might have been caused by a couple of ducks!

The monster legend was on its way though, supported by more sightings and some photographs. The most famous of the photos was taken in 1934 by a London surgeon, and it convinced many people of the monster's reality. But perhaps notice should have been taken of the photo's date: 1 April.

Over the years that followed hundreds of people claimed to have seen the monster. Unfortunately, eye-witnesses differed about its appearance and size.

It was black, grey or mottled. No it wasn't, it was mahogany-coloured – or even white!

It was huge – or it was quite small. It had one hump – or two – or three. It had horns – or it didn't have horns. It had legs and was seen on land, or it had flippers and never left the water.

Many of the sightings were dismissed, even by monster enthusiasts. Otters, deer, birds, floating logs, the wakes of boats and even hump-shaped rocks all delude people into believing that they've caught sight of Nessie. Loch Ness is also subject to mirage effects, especially in the early morning, when most sightings occur.

But a few were by trustworthy observers, such as Father Gregory Brusey. In 1971 he and a companion were by the edge of the loch when suddenly a huge beast reared up out of the water! The men would not have made a story up, so what did they see: an otter enlarged by the mirage effect, or a fearsome creature from the depths?

If it was a monster, what kind of beast was it? The most popular idea was that it was a plesiosaurus, left over from the age of the dinosaurs. Never mind that scientists said that plesiosauruses were sea creatures and

24

died out seventy million years ago: scientists had said that the fish called a coelacanth was extinct, yet one was caught alive in 1938, and others have been caught since.

But if there was a breeding colony of plesiosauruses trapped in the loch when the exit to the sea closed up and which then adapted to the fresh water, why were no bones discovered when divers searched the bottom for them?

In 1962 the Loch Ness Phenomena Investigation Bureau was formed, supported by well-known people such as the naturalist Sir Peter Scott. Sophisticated cameras and underwater sonar equipment were employed, and hundreds of people joined in an annual series of loch-watches.

Nothing definite was found. A mysterious distant moving object was captured on film, and there were a few inexplicable underwater movements recorded by sonar scan, but it was a poor reward for so much effort.

The greatest excitement came in 1975 when an American, Robert Rines, obtained underwater photographs which he said proved the monster's existence. He and Sir Peter Scott gave it a scientific name – *Nessiteras rhombopteryx* (the Ness monster with diamond-shaped fin). It was unfortunate for them that some wit realized that an anagram of the new name was 'Monster hoax by Sir Peter S'!

Perhaps investigators built up too-high hopes over these photographs. When they were published they seemed too indistinct to be 'the final proof'. The photograph of a fin, claimed to be two metres long, had nothing to give a sense of scale: it might belong to a huge creature, but there again, as Sir David Attenborough pointed out, it might be the fin of quite a small fish.

Since then Nessie-sightings have been few and far between. Believers have become a dwindling band.

The summer of 1992 brought enthusiasts a glimmer of hope, however. Project Urquhart is a new scientific investigation of the loch and more interested in finding microscopic worms than monsters. But there was excitement when for a whole two minutes sonar contact was made with something underwater which was larger and stronger than any single fish. Loch Ness has no fish shoals, so what else could have produced the echo? Could there, after all, be a monster in the loch?

6

Was Constance a Killer?

In 1865 a twenty-one-year-old girl, Constance Kent, confessed to the murder five years earlier of her stepbrother, Francis Savile Kent. The four-year-old boy had been taken from his cot, his throat slashed so viciously that his head was almost cut off, and his body thrust down the outside privy. (A privy is a toilet built over a hole.)

Because Constance had only been sixteen at the time of the crime she was reprieved from the gallows. She served twenty years' penal servitude, then on release emigrated to Australia and slipped into obscurity.

But did she do it? The chances are that, despite her confession, she paid a terrible price for a crime of which she was totally innocent.

Constance's version of events was that she had secreted a razor from her father's shaving-set, then on the night of the murder had taken the child from his cot, carried him

downstairs and climbed with him – still asleep – through the drawing-room window, then to the privy where she cut his throat.

Her motive for this brutal cruelty was, she said, revenge for remarks made by her stepmother about her own family.

The Kents lived in a large house in Wiltshire, and Samuel Kent, the father, was an inspector of factories in the West of England. After his first wife's death he had married his children's nurse, who then treated these children of the earlier marriage unkindly. Constance in particular was bullied, and often locked in a cellar.

Yet the evidence suggests that she didn't bear a grudge against her stepmother's children, and that she was, in fact, very fond of Savile. She had been playing with him on the day of his death, and he was making her a necklace.

As for her account of the crime, it doesn't make sense. No one could have caused that appalling injury with just a razor, even a Victorian 'cut-throat' one. It was only possible to open the sash-window about fifteen centimetres – how could Constance have got herself and a child through the gap without waking him? Why use the window when she could have gone out of the back door?

The police investigation at the time was, unfortunately, bungled. Mr Kent was determined that neither he nor his wife were going to be questioned. When a blood-stained night-dress was found pushed up a chimney, Mr Kent persuaded the police to leave it there to watch for the criminal coming back for it – then he locked them in the kitchen! Naturally when he let them out again the evidence had gone.

Because a muddle with the laundry suggested that the night-dress might have been hers, Constance was arrested. But for lack of any evidence the case was thrown out. The slur of suspicion had, however, been fastened on her.

The police then arrested the nursemaid. It was hard to believe that a child could be taken from a room where she also slept without her waking up – particularly since the door squeaked. It was thought that she might have been entertaining a lover, who killed Savile when he woke and saw them. However, this unsupported case was dismissed too.

But what if the lover was the boy's father, Samuel Kent? He had had an affair with his first wife's nurse: was history repeating itself?

If Mr Kent was making love to the nurse when the

child woke up he could have panicked at the prospect of discovery (Savile was known as a tell-tale), and throttled him. Medical examination showed that Savile had been suffocated before his throat was cut, though the police never seem to have thought about what this implied.

If Mr Kent did in panic or blind fury murder his son then, with the help of the nurse, he had to make it look as if a vicious outsider had got into the house.

The case got no further until Constance's extraordinary confession. Could there be a reason why she should have confessed to something she did not do?

Constance was then herself training to be a nurse. She was in a religious institution where pressure was put on her to 'confess'. In the intense atmosphere, and with no friends to turn to for advice, she perhaps felt that God wished her to be the scapegoat for the crime. It is known that when she saw her father after the confession she told him that she'd done it 'for you and God'.

Some, however, still think that no one would have confessed to such a terrible crime if they didn't do it. It has been suggested that Constance did throttle Savile, but was discovered by her father. He then staged the rest of the grisly business to avoid family scandal.

We cannot ever know what was really locked in Constance's heart. But we can agree with the inscription on little Savile's grave that he was most 'cruelly murdered'.

7

The Giant Picture-book
of Nazca

In the Nazca desert of southern Peru you can find the largest picture-gallery in the world. But this is no ordinary display of art: the drawings, a whole zoo of animals and birds, are of monster size, laid out on the desert floor.

A giant condor has a wing-span of more than 120 metres; a lurking spider is nearly fifty metres long. There's a humming-bird with a vast bill, a curly-tailed monkey, a splashing whale, and many more birds, fishes, and strange plant forms.

Because of their size, you can't really see the pictures at ground level. Only when airborne can you appreciate the whole wriggling, flying menagerie.

They are highly stylized outlines, resembling the shapes which decorate the pottery of the Indians who lived around Nazca from before the time of Christ to about AD 900.

They were made by the simple, if laborious, method of removing the dark stone layer which covers the desert, or pampa, and revealing the light-coloured sand beneath. The geometric accuracy of the designs was probably achieved by skilful scaling up of much smaller versions.

Another extraordinary feature of the pampa would have required the same high degree of skill: a vast network of straight lines which criss-cross it. They march for miles, never deviating in their straightness, no matter what rocky hill or valley gets in the way. There are also enormous rectangles, triangles, spirals, and 400-metre-long 'arrows'.

Though archaeologists knew about the lines, the pictures were not discovered till 1941. An American, Paul Kosok, was plotting some curious twisting lines, when to his amazement he found that they formed the outline of a giant condor.

Since then his assistant, a dedicated German woman called Maria Reiche, has given her life to finding, recording and protecting the pictures. They weren't easy to spot, since the desert winds had blown a thin dark layer of pebbles over the markings. Maria had herself lashed to a plank under a helicopter to help locate the outlines. Once one was found she would take a broom and painstakingly sweep it clean again.

The big puzzle is: why did the Nazcas draw giant pictures in the sand which they couldn't see properly?

Perhaps they were for the gods, not humans, to see: most have connections in Indian mythology with water, so they could have formed a kind of prayer for rain.

Some have suggested that they were intended to be walked in ritual fashion, because if you were to begin at an 'entry' point, it would be possible to travel round the outline of the pictures in one continuous movement, twisting and turning as in a maze.

However, Jim Woodman, an American, was convinced that the Indians themselves must have been able to see their creations. In 1975 he set out to prove that they could have flown in hot-air balloons. Using only materials which would have been available to the Nazcas, he made a balloon, filled it with smoky heat from a giant bonfire, and with an English co-pilot successfully lifted off on a short flight.

But even if he had proved the possibility of early flight (and some people felt he had only proved that it would have been very dangerous), the reasons for flying and viewing the drawings remained obscure. Woodman suggested that perhaps the Nazcas gave their chieftains a sky 'burial'.

What, if any, is the connection between the pictures and the lines? Some join with lines; others are partly lost because lines have been taken right over them.

What makes the lines so difficult to explain is that there are so many of them, and they differ so much in length, width and direction. All kinds of suggestions for their use have been made, including some lunatic ones: they were landing-strips for alien spacecraft; they were used for Olympic-type games; the rectangles were areas for giant weaving looms.

More reasonably it has been argued that they had religious significance. Maria Reiche thinks they line up with sun, moon and stars to form an astronomical calendar. Others have suggested that alignments with heavenly bodies would have helped farmers to know when to plant crops. Almost certainly some are just what they seem: paths for crossing the desert.

These marvellous monuments continue to intrigue and tantalize us. Sadly, though, they are very fragile, and careless tourists have damaged a number of them. Now, the Peruvian government has banned anyone from the area where the best pictures are. Ironically, therefore, the world's biggest display of art can now *only* be seen from the air.

8

How Many Lives do we Lead?

A journalist on the *Independent* newspaper not long ago described a hypnosis session in which he seemed to remember several past lives. As a non-believer in reincarnation – the idea that each human spirit has many different existences – he was surprised to find himself recalling lives as a farmer in William the Conqueror's reign, as an Elizabethan landowner, and as a hat-maker in Victorian times.

Though he decided that all these 'lives' had developed from his own knowledge of history, he was startled by the vividness of the pictures in his mind.

Interest in reincarnation, an accepted part of Eastern religions such as Hinduism and Buddhism, has grown this century in the Western world, and there are some

strange stories which seem to support it.

As a small child Reena Gupta of Delhi, born in 1966, was always spending time on the balcony of her home, looking at the crowds below 'for her children'. She told her mother that she had had four children, but that her husband, 'a very bad man', had killed her. Some years later her mother heard of a Sikh family that seemed to tally with Reena's tales. In 1961 the mother of four had been murdered and the husband served a prison sentence.

Without telling Reena where they were going her mother took her to the house of the parents of the murdered wife. When Reena saw them she cried excitedly, 'They are my mother and father.' She also joyfully greeted the four children (all older than her!). But, forced to meet the father, she was terrified, and reluctant to pose for a photograph with him.

Two-year-old Jeremy Anderson, born in Oklahoma in 1975, kept insisting that his name was Jimmy and that he had been 'killed' in a road accident. In fact, his father had had a half-brother, James Houser, who was killed while joy-riding with a friend in 1967. Taken when five years old to the place where Jimmy had lived, Jeremy seemed to recognize his surroundings and remembered with distress his high-speed crash into a truck.

There are many other cases where young children appear to recall previous lives, though fortunately they usually forget about them by the age of ten and get on with their 'new' ones.

Adults are generally brought to remember past 'lives' through hypnosis. One woman came to terms with her fear of flying after remembering being shot down in flames as a pilot in the Second World War. Of course, disbelievers in reincarnation would say that hypnosis merely enabled the woman to invent a comforting story to explain her anxieties.

Other stories have been explained away too. A case which hit the headlines in the 1950s was that of an American woman who recalled in amazing detail a life as a nineteenth-century Irishwoman, 'Bridey Murphy'. But doubts set in when it was discovered that as a child she had had a neighbour called 'Bridey', and that an aunt could have told her tales about Ireland. Even so, the details and the dialect she used seemed extraordinary.

No one has been able easily to dismiss the 'past lives', tape-recorded under hypnosis, of a Welsh woman known as Jane Evans to protect her real identity. With impressive historical accuracy she appeared to recall seven different existences from the fifth to the twentieth century.

One of her lives was as 'Rebecca', a woman living in twelfth-century York, who was apparently persecuted for her Jewish faith. The tape ends with Rebecca's terror as a murderous mob break into the church crypt where she is in hiding with her daughter.

Rebecca's story was checked by an expert who could find no errors in its historical detail, except that it was thought that the church in which she took refuge had no crypt. Yet six months later workmen in the church broke through a wall and discovered such a crypt.

Another of Jane Evans's lives was as 'Alison', serving girl to a French nobleman of the fifteenth century, Jacques Coeur. She worked for him in a grand house in Bourges, which Jane Evans described accurately, though she had never been to Bourges. And she would have found it impossible to have read in detail in English about Jacques Coeur's life.

Of course, no story provides proof of reincarnation. Doubters wonder why more of us don't remember, at least in childhood, the lives we're supposed to have led in the past. Where do the genetics which make us like our parents come into it? And what about the increase in population? Are new 'spirits' constantly being formed? Or are we being recycled faster and faster?

But if reincarnation is pure fantasy then stories like Jane Evans's show at least that we are a long way yet from understanding the intricacies of the human mind.

9

Who Was Anastasia?

My name was Fräulein Unbekannt. But you can call me Anna, though my friends call me Anastasia ...Er...Actually my official title is Grand Duchess...er...

On the night of 17 February 1920 a young woman was pulled from the dark waters of a canal in Berlin into which she had jumped. But when questioned she would not speak, or even give her name.

Weeks later, still unidentified, she was sent to a lunatic asylum. There she was called Fräulein Unbekannt (Miss Unknown).

Doctors were soon sure that she was not insane, just terrified of recognition. They also saw on her arms and legs the scars of hideous injuries, and damage to the side of her head which suggested a bullet wound.

For more than a year Fräulein Unbekannt lived among the mentally ill. Then suddenly she announced her true identity as that of the Russian Grand Duchess Anastasia, youngest daughter of Czar Nicholas II and the Empress Alexandra!

But Anastasia was believed to have perished with her

parents, three sisters and brother in July 1918. At that time, during the Russian Revolution, the royal family was imprisoned by the Bolsheviks (hard-line Communists) in a house in Ekaterinberg in Siberia. According to later investigators all the family and their servants were shot and bayoneted in the cellar and their bodies destroyed. Anastasia would then have been seventeen.

How, if she was really Anastasia, had she escaped? (To avoid confusion we had better call her Anna: Anna Anderson was the name she adopted later for legal identity.)

Anna said that after the massacre she was found alive and rescued by Alexander Tchaikovsky, a young man sent to clear away the bodies. For weeks, ill and distressed, she was jolted in a peasant's cart on a long journey to Bucharest in Romania. All Alexander's family escaped with them and they lived off the jewels stitched into her underclothes.

She bore a son and married Alexander, but he was killed while trading one of the jewels. Anna then decided to go to Berlin to find her relations, leaving the child with its grandmother. Alexander's brother went with her, but once there he disappeared. She had then despaired.

Anna's tale was unprovable, so what suggested that she might indeed be Anastasia?

First was the physical resemblance. The facial structure was much the same, and she also had startling blue eyes, which reminded everyone who had met him of Nicholas II.

Anna had a crooked finger just as Anastasia had, following an accident with a coach door. She also had the same deformation of the feet, with the same foot worse than the other.

There was her detailed knowledge of Anastasia's life,

and her temperament too, which was very much that of a Grand Duchess, both in the good sense that she had the grace and dignity expected of royalty, but also in the less pleasing way in which she could be very difficult and demanding.

Probably it was this tricky temperament that cost her recognition. Anna didn't see why she should have to work to persuade people who she was. When Anastasia's aunt, Irene of Prussia, came to see her, she came under an assumed name. Anna was bewildered and furious that her aunt should pretend to be someone else. She refused to speak to her or to indicate that she knew who it was.

Her aunt was equally offended and, though admitting a likeness, she would not acknowledge Anna as her niece, or come again.

Those who took the trouble to gain Anna's confidence almost always ended by accepting her as Anastasia, but the people who counted, Anastasia's close relations, were uniformly hostile. They based their opposition largely on the testimony of one man, Pierre Gilliard, the former Swiss tutor to the royal family, who became the most vehement of Anna's opponents.

He said that she did not look like Anastasia, that she spoke no Russian, only German, which Anastasia had never learnt, that she didn't remember things which Anastasia would know, and would not answer his questions about Siberia.

However, he saw her when she was very ill and he made no allowance for the psychological trauma which would have made a real Anastasia very reluctant to talk about her ordeal.

He was wrong about the Russian – Anna could not speak Russian because, she said, of her terrible memories, but she understood the language very well, and sometimes spoke it. Later discovery of Anastasia's lesson books proved that she had in fact learnt German, as Gilliard must have known.

Anna spent nearly fifty years trying in the courts to establish her identity, until too old to care any more. She married an American and found some happiness before her death in 1984.

Postscript: In 1991 nine skeletons were found in a pit in Siberia which are almost certainly those of the Tsar, his family, and loyal servants killed with them. British forensic scientists have been asked to test the bones for DNA genetic material which should prove their identity, and it is reported that they are also testing hair belonging to Anna Anderson, since no skeleton was found in the pit which could be hers. By the time this book is published we may well know whether Anna was of imperial blood as she claimed, or not. If she was, it's too late to do her any good!

10

The Cheltenham Ghost

The case in 1991 of a New York couple getting their money back when they found that the house they wanted to buy was haunted reminds us that ghosts aren't found only in crumbling old mansions. They can turn up anywhere and have even been known to move house them-

selves – that at least seems to have happened in the curious case of the Cheltenham ghost.

This ghost is very well authenticated. It was seen by a large number of people, and its activities were carefully recorded by a fearless young ghost-buster of the 1880s, Rosina Despard.

Rosina's father, Captain Despard, had moved with his family into a large house in Cheltenham in April 1882. Apart from nineteen-year-old Rosina there was an older married daughter, three younger daughters and two sons.

One night in June Rosina thought she heard her mother at her bedroom door. Candle in hand she went to open it, but instead of her mother she saw 'the figure of a tall lady, dressed in black, standing at the head of the stairs'. The woman's face was hidden in a handkerchief held in her right hand.

After a few moments the figure turned and went downstairs. Rosina followed until her candle suddenly burnt out.

During the next two years Rosina saw the figure several times though she discussed it only with a friend. But others began to have strange encounters too.

Rosina's married sister, on a visit, wondered who the nun was whose back view she glimpsed going into the drawing-room. But no one was found within. The younger son and a friend were in the garden when they caught sight of a lady crying in the drawing-room. But again when they asked a servant who it was they were told the room was empty.

Once a neighbour sent across to inquire about a woman seen crying bitterly in the orchard – she was described as tall, dressed like a widow, and with a hanky to her face.

Most of the Despard family and some of the servants saw the figure at one time or another – though never when they were looking for it. And everyone could hear the footsteps and rattling doorknobs.

The maids were terrified to leave their rooms at night, but resourceful Rosina stretched cords across the stairs to test the ghost (it glided through), tried to touch it (it vanished), and to speak to it (it didn't reply).

Then after four years the figure was seen less often till finally it disappeared for good, and even the noises stopped.

Whose ghost was it? The house was quite new; its only previous owner was a solicitor called Henry Swinhoe. The ghostly figure was believed by Rosina to be that of his second wife, Imogen. This marriage had been very unhappy, which explained, to Rosina's satisfaction, why the figure was crying.

Perhaps there wasn't a ghost at all? The Society for Psychical Research, set up in 1882 to investigate reports of hauntings, considered whether the mysterious figure was a real woman, kept secretly in the house by Captain Despard. But that, they decided, would have been impossible.

The Society was impressed by the large number of people who claimed to have seen the ghost – about seventeen in all – and by the business-like attitude of Rosina (who later qualified as a doctor, one of the few Victorian women to do so).

One commentator, trying to find a rational explanation, suggested that the surgings of an underground stream could have caused the rattling doorknobs and apparent footsteps. In this case people might have seen a figure because the sounds led them to expect one.

In 1886 Cheltenham's new reservoirs came into use, and they would have trapped the underground waters, thus ending the noises. But ingenious though this theory is, it doesn't account for all the sightings.

And then there is the business of the ghost's reappearance elsewhere. In 1961 William Thorne of Maidenhead visited his brother, whose flat was in a house on the other side of the road from the Despards' old home. Mr Thorne and his fifteen-year-old son John had gone to bed when Mr Thorne heard footsteps ouside the room. Thinking it was his sister-in-law he called out her name – but at the open door appeared a black-clad figure, outlined in phosphorescence, with a hanky to its face.

John woke up and saw the ghostly vision too. He was not afraid, and when his (more cowardly?) father told him to go and shut the door he got up to do so. Immediately the figure vanished. Next day they discovered that John's uncle had had a similar fright one night.

Perhaps the unhappy ghost had got fed up with Rosina's trip-wires and questioning, and went off to find a more desirable residence to carry on its haunting. If so, it will have had to move again, as that house has now been demolished.

11

A Burning Question

WARNING : Smoking can damage your health

Nineteen-year-old Vicky Gilmour was lucky. At a disco in Darlington (County Durham) in 1980 she suddenly and inexplicably burst into flames. She survived – unlike poor Jacqueline Fitzsimon, five years later. She was a cookery student in Widnes (Cheshire) and on 28 January she had taken an exam and was chatting with friends afterwards on the college stairs.

Suddenly she cried out, 'My back's gone hot – am I on fire? I'm on fire!' before being engulfed by flame.

In both cases extensive tests on the girls' clothing failed to reproduce conditions which could have led to such sudden, terrifying burning. It is likely that they were victims of what is known as 'spontaneous human combustion' (SHC), where it seems that the blaze actually begins within the body.

Puzzling cases of what was once called 'fire from heaven' have been noted for at least four centuries. As the name suggests it was once seen as God's punishment for misdeeds.

In the last century it was thought that victims were alcoholics, who blazed up as human torches because their tissues were saturated with drink. Dickens, in his novel *Bleak House*, has an evil old gin-soaked character called Krook who dies horribly this way.

But we now know that alcohol is not to blame, though we are no nearer understanding the real cause. Moreover, it isn't officially recognized as a cause of death. As with Jacqueline Fitzsimon, coroners usually insist on a verdict of 'death by misadventure'.

But at least in the cases of the two girls the fires, if they were 'spontaneous', did not take the full grisly course often recorded.

What makes SHC so spine-chilling is that the bodies of the victims are frequently reduced to little more than piles of ash. For the human body this is normally impossible – even after twelve hours of burning at 1,650 degrees centigrade recognizable pieces of bone should remain.

Yet in SHC cases the devastating heat which totally destroys the bodies causes almost no other fire damage.

The first case to be thoroughly investigated by a forensic scientist was the death of elderly Mrs Mary Reeser in 1951 in Florida. When her body was discovered it had been reduced to no more than a pile of ash – except for one foot still incongruously clad in a black satin slipper.

Astonishingly, the only other thing to have burnt was

the chair Mrs Reeser had been sitting on. Newspapers and other inflammable objects nearby had not caught light.

Dr Wilton Krogman, the professor who spent months investigating the circumstances of Mrs Reeser's death, could not explain it. It was, he said, 'the most amazing thing any of us ever saw'.

A similar case in Pennsylvania occurred on 5 December 1966. Don Gosnall called to read the gas meter at the home of ninety-two-year-old Dr John Bentley. The door was unlocked and he let himself in, noticing a strange sweet smell and a bluish haze. On the floor of the basement he saw a small pile of ash.

After reading the meter Mr Gosnall went upstairs to find Dr Bentley. In the bathroom he made a gruesome discovery: all that remained of the old man was the ash which had fallen through a burnt hole in the floor, and part of a leg. Grotesquely tilted over the hole was Dr Bentley's walking-frame.

Again a fire of presumably inferno heat had left the house almost undamaged. Little wonder that scientists are baffled.

There have, of course, been attempts to explain the phenomenon. Suggestions include the effects of the earth's magnetic field, or a kind of internal lightning strike. In truth, however, there is no convincing explanation.

As we have seen, some fortunate victims have lived to tell the tale. One freezing January day in 1835 an American Professor, James Hamilton, felt a sharp stinging pain in his left leg. Looking down he saw a jet of flame spurting out. With considerable presence of mind he slapped his hand on his leg and kept it there till the flame was extinguished.

More recently, in May 1985, nineteen-year-old Paul King was walking in a London street late at night when he burst into flames. He collapsed on the pavement in intense pain, but luckily the flames evaporated as mysteriously as they had begun. Though badly burnt, he too survived.

Statistically it is, of course, very unlikely that any one person will die of spontaneous combustion. But the two hundred or so recorded cases like those of Mrs Reeser and Dr Bentley make SHC very difficult to dismiss as alarmist fantasy.

12

Mary Queen of Scots

At two o'clock in the morning of 10 February 1567 the people of Edinburgh were woken by a shattering noise: a huge gunpowder explosion had reduced Kirk o' Field, a house on the edge of the town, to rubble. Staying in it was Henry Stuart, Lord Darnley, the husband of Mary, Queen of Scotland.

But Lord Darnley had not been blown to pieces by the blast. Instead, his body was found, with that of a servant, in a nearby garden. They had been strangled. Presumably Darnley had heard suspicious noises and was trying to flee, but in a white night-gown was easily spotted by his assassins.

Was Mary Queen of Scots herself involved in the murder?

She had good reason to hate Darnley. The beautiful and vivacious young woman had at one time been both Queen of Scotland in her own right and Queen of France through marriage, but after being widowed she had returned to Scotland. In 1565 she chose her cousin Darnley as her second husband – at nineteen he was three years her junior.

Darnley was good-looking but, as Mary soon discovered, a handsome appearance hid an ugly nature. Though pleased to find herself pregnant with an heir, Mary turned away from Darnley and gave her confidence instead to her Italian secretary, David Rizzio. This favouritism aroused a jealous fury in Darnley.

One evening Mary was having supper with friends, including Rizzio, in a small room in Holyrood Palace. Suddenly Darnley and his henchmen burst in. Though he clung to Mary's skirts, Rizzio was dragged away screaming and brutally murdered, while a pistol was held to Mary's stomach.

Mary never forgave her husband for this outrage.

Although her son, James, was safely born three months later, she wanted to be rid of the baby's father.

Mary's problem was that divorce as we know it was impossible. She might be able to get her marriage declared null and void, but that would also make her son illegitimate and rob him of his right to inherit the throne.

The Queen told her nobles that nothing must be done contrary to her honour and conscience, but she must have known that the only way to secure both legitimacy for her son and Darnley's removal as her husband, was with his death.

Chief amongst her supporters was James Hepburn, Earl of Bothwell. With the same kind of blindness that made her choose first Darnley and then Rizzio, she put her trust in Bothwell, who was quick to set his own ambitious schemes in motion.

In January 1567 Darnley fell ill. Surprisingly, Mary showed herself concerned about him. They had been living apart, but now she persuaded him to come with her to Edinburgh, promising to be a loving wife to him again when he recovered.

Darnley himself chose Kirk o' Field as his lodging, and there he was frequently visited by Mary. On the fateful evening she had intended to stay overnight until she suddenly remembered an entertainment she wanted to attend at Holyrood Palace. When she heard of the 'horrible and strange' events that followed, Mary declared 'it was not chance but God that put it in our head'.

Was Mary lying? Did she deliberately lull Darnley into a false sense of security to help the murderers?

Her behaviour sounds very suspicious, and many people were as sure that she was involved as that Bothwell was principal murderer. Mary didn't help belief in her innocence by her calm attendance at a wedding celebration next day.

But it's never been proved. Mary's supporters argue that her apparent change of heart towards Darnley, though put on, was because she'd heard that he was plotting against *her*. She wanted him where she could keep an eye on him. After all, he had carried out the cold-blooded murder of Rizzio.

Maybe Mary's actions simply provided Bothwell and the other conspirators with their opportunity. But whether she knew of the plans or not, the murder led Mary rapidly to catastrophe.

First she was abducted by Bothwell and forced to marry him. This prompted others of her lords to rebel and she was made to abdicate in favour of the baby James. She was then imprisoned in the island castle of Lochleven.

Her escape from Lochleven a year later is a stirring story, but it did Mary no good. She sought sanctuary in England, but even though she was Queen Elizabeth I's closest relative she was kept a prisoner. After eighteen years of imprisonment she foolishly allowed herself to get caught up in a plot against Elizabeth, was found guilty of treason and executed.

It was a sad end to a disastrous life. But Mary and Darnley did achieve one thing between them: after Elizabeth I's death their son James became King of England, uniting Scotland and England, thus ending centuries of rivalry and bloodshed.

13

The Devil's Footprints

The trouble with most strange events is that they are witnessed by so few people. But in the case of the bizarre footprints in South Devon in 1855, virtually everyone living around the estuary of the River Exe saw them.

That winter had been a particularly severe one. Roads and rivers froze over, even in the mild South West. Then on the night of 8 February it snowed. Some people afterwards said that dogs had barked inexplicably in the night, but most were unaware that anything extraordinary had happened till the morning.

Then they saw a line of footprints, running up to their doors, crossing their gardens, traversing orchards, fields and farmyards. Scarcely a place remained unvisited. The prints were like a donkey's – but what donkey can leap on to a roof and leave its tracks right across it? They crossed haystacks too, ran along the tops of walls, or stopped on one side of a high wall and started again on the other.

Moreover, they were in a single line, as if a two-footed beast had been taking a midnight walk. And what a walk! The creature had covered a hundred miles in its travels. Alarmingly, some of the prints seemed to be cloven, and burnt into the ice. It was no wonder that many of the country folk said that the Devil had been abroad that night.

The story reached the London papers, and soon many people were adding their observations and speculating about the cause.

Looking at the reports and letters we can see that the true facts are not quite the same as the legend just told, though still very mysterious.

In the first place the footprints didn't form a continuous line. They stopped and started, sometimes appearing in the middle of a field. A party of men who tried to track the mystery beast ended back where they'd begun. Secondly, not all observers noted a single line of prints. Many reported a parallel line of tracks.

It seems likely that some prints were made by hoaxers after the original discovery. The congregation of the village of Woodford was still seething about the new and, in their view, irreligious carols they'd been forced to sing at Christmas (one of these objectionable carols was 'Good King Wenceslas'!). No surprise then, if someone had the bright idea of burning the Devil's footprints with a red-hot donkey's shoe up to the vestry door (their own prints wouldn't have shown up on the hardened ice).

But, even allowing for modifications to the usually-reported tale, we are left to identify an animal that can fly like a bird yet makes tracks like a donkey.

Numerous suggestions were made at the time, such as a high-hopping kangaroo (one had escaped from a zoo), otters, cats, rats (jumping and landing with four feet together). One writer thought it was toads, because it was the mating season. (Would they have come out in all that snow and ice?) Prints which disappeared down a narrow pipe and reappeared at the other end must surely have belonged to some small mammal.

Richard Owen, the famous biologist who first named the dinosaurs, said that the print of which he'd been sent a drawing had undoubtedly been made by a badger. But badgers couldn't have made the marks over house roofs.

A clergyman discovered some 'devil's droppings' (small, round and whitish) and sent them to Owen for analysis – what he made of them is unfortunately not recorded!

Two cranes were shot in the estuary, and it was thought they might have been responsible, or perhaps large wader birds. But no one was very confident that they could make marks like a donkey.

The mystery remains unsolved, though people still make guesses. A recently-offered theory is that a secret experimental balloon broke loose from Devonport dock-yard, trailing iron shackles which made the marks. But it is very unlikely that a balloon could have created the regularly-spaced prints that everybody noticed.

If one wants a natural rather than a supernatural explanation then it is probable that several creatures were involved – maybe even a genuine donkey contributed! Surely only birds could have made the roof- and wall-top marks, and one idea is that ice on birds' feet might have disguised their true shape. But it's odd that no one heard heavy-footed birds flapping and thumping over roofs, nor saw them in the daytime.

Postscript: In the hard winter of 1963 a West Country woman woke to find six donkey-like prints in her front garden, and six more in the back even though there was no way between except over the roof. So, if it snows and you live near the River Exe, watch out for flying donkeys!

14

The Lost Expedition

A haunting question asked in the middle of the last century was what had happened to the expedition, led by Sir John Franklin, to the icy waters of the Canadian Arctic. Even today we puzzle the loss of the two ships, 125 men and four boys.

For hundreds of years it had been a dream to find a north-west passage, a sea-route around northern Canada, and many sailors' lives were lost in the slow charting of these northerly waters. In 1845 Sir John Franklin, a seasoned polar explorer, was aiming to finish the task and make the first voyage through into the Pacific.

The voyage was expected to last at least three years, and the two ships, the *Erebus* and the *Terror*, were well provisioned. On top of other essentials the holds were packed with 8,000 tins of meat, soup and vegetables.

Preserving food in tins was a recent invention which had helped to make such expeditions possible.

When the ships set sail on 5 May 1845 a dove settled on a mast, and it seemed a happy omen. In the days before radio nobody expected to hear much news, though later that year two whalers brought back cheerful messages. But from then on – silence.

By the end of 1847 people were beginning to worry and search-parties were dispatched. Horrifying rumours were picked up from the Inuit of starvation and even cannibalism amongst white men. But not till 1850 was anything definite discovered.

Then a campsite, used during the expedition's first winter, was found. Remnants of clothing and piles of used tins lay around. Also nearby were three carefully-made graves: of John Torrington, aged 20, who died 1 January 1846, John Hartnell, aged 25, died 4 January

1846, and William Braine, aged 32, died 3 April 1846. It seemed ominous that three young men had died so early on in the expedition.

In 1854 Franklin's wife, Lady Jane, appealed to the British public to help her finance one last search expedition. £3,000 was raised – a large sum in those days – and in 1859 Captain Francis M'Clintock set off north to see what he could find.

M'Clintock explored King William Island, the only unmapped territory and not even known to be an island. There he found a cairn containing a piece of naval paper. On it were two scribbled notes, both signed by Franklin officers. One recorded a successful first year and noted 'All well'.

But the second told a different tale. Dated 25 April 1848, it tersely recorded the deaths of Sir John Franklin and twenty-four others. It went on to say that the remaining men were abandoning their ships after nineteen months trapped in unrelenting ice. They planned to trek south to the Great Fish River in Canada.

A little further on M'Clintock came on a lifeboat mounted on a sledge. In it were skeletons, guns, and also, strangely, things like scented soap, silk handkerchiefs, button polish and curtain rods. In their desperate situation, why did the men bother burdening themselves with such useless objects?

Later in the century the story was taken further when more grim remains were found on the Canadian mainland, at a place afterwards known as Starvation Cove.

It was clear, therefore, that Sir John Franklin's team did in the end complete the map and find the North-West Passage. But his men paid with their lives for the knowledge that what they thought a peninsula was an island.

Had he only guessed this, Franklin could have travelled down the eastern, less hostile, coast, and then sailed home triumphantly.

But why, on a well-provisioned expedition, did so many men die before that last desperate trek? One possible reason has been suggested by a Canadian, Dr Owen Beattie.

In 1984 he got permission to exhume the three 1846 graves. His party first dug down through the frozen ground of the youngest man's grave, 20-year-old John Torrington. When the coffin was opened the body was found completely frozen in a block of ice. They gently thawed it with hot water and were moved to see a well-preserved, youthful face.

Beattie took samples of nails, hair and body tissue back to Canada for analysis. There it was discovered that Torrington – though he'd died of TB and pneumonia – had been suffering from lead-poisoning. This later proved true of the other men also.

The new technique of tinning food had probably also led to disaster. Food must have been contaminated by the lead solder which sealed the tins. The consequent slow poisoning would have weakened the men and impaired their judgement.

No trace has ever been found of the abandoned ships. But in 1851 a merchant ship, the *Renovation*, was sailing to Quebec when, near Newfoundland, it met with huge, towering icebergs. On one was a fantastic sight: two apparently undamaged ships locked into the ice. Though 2,000 miles from where they had been anchored, it is probable that they were *Erebus* and *Terror*, still trapped by the ice which had brought despair and death to their crews.

15

Vanishing Acts

When world-weary Hamlet in Shakespeare's play cries 'O that this too, too solid flesh would melt' he doesn't expect it to happen. But a number of strange stories are told of people who seem, literally, to melt into thin air. Can they be true?

Two such cases occurred in 1975, for example, one in America, one in England.

On a snowy February day of that year Mr and Mrs Wright were driving to New York. Snow built up on the front and rear windscreens, so when they got to the Lincoln Tunnel Mr Wright stopped the car. He attended to the front windscreen while his wife, Martha, took a cloth to the rear. But when Mr Wright looked up Martha had vanished. She has never been seen again.

Donald Dent disappeared in the summer-time. He lived near Newmarket in Cambridgeshire, and worked at a stud farm. On 5 June he stayed at home from work with a sore throat.

In the evening he sat in the living-room watching television and his wife brought him his supper. Later Mrs Dent looked in on her husband and told him she was going to bed. He promised to follow at the end of the TV programme. But he didn't come. When she went downstairs she expected to find him asleep in a chair – but though the TV was still on the room was empty. Despite a widespread search over several days no trace was ever found of Donald Dent.

The earlier case of nineteen-year-old Alex Cleghorn was even more peculiar. As reported in 1966 in the *Scottish Daily Express*, he vanished in full view of his two brothers. On New Year's Eve the three of them were walking down Govan Road in Glasgow, on their way to the usual celebrations, when Alex simply disappeared from between them! To all knowledge he has never been seen again.

These sorts of story lead some commentators to suggest abduction by aliens, or that there is some kind of equivalent to the 'black holes' of outer space around us. But, of course, there could be natural explanations for the disappearances.

Perhaps Martha Wright wanted to leave her husband and chose this odd moment to do so; maybe Donald Dent suffered amnesia, left home undetected and somehow avoided later discovery. Alex's brothers might have made up their stories – perhaps Alex wanted to do a bunk and his brothers thought of a spine-chilling way to cover it. Or maybe the newspaper just got the story wrong.

In dealing with mysteries and reading about them one has to be very careful not to accept everything at face value. Mystery writers want to intrigue their readers, and sometimes make too much of a story. The next often-told tale is a case in point.

In September 1880, it is said, David Lang, who worked a farm on the Old Cottontown Road in Summer County, Tennessee, was walking across one of his fields. He was going to meet his brother-in-law, Judge August Peck, whose horse and buggy were drawing near. His wife and children stood on the porch of their farmhouse watching and waving.

But then, in full view of all his relatives and in the middle of the open field, David Lang vanished. The ground had not given way. Despite frantic searching nothing could be discovered of the unfortunate farmer's fate.

This story became widely known following publication in a magazine in 1953 and there is so much precise detail that the shocked reader feels it must be true.

But one local man decided to look into it. Hershel G. Payne was a librarian, so it was easy for him to consult the records.

He could find no reference to a David Lang, nor could he locate the supposed farm in Cottontown Road. A judge is a distinguished figure and ought to be traceable, but no Judge Peck was recorded. Yet, despite the doubts Payne's discoveries throw on the story, the mysterious disappearance of Farmer Lang keeps reappearing in books.

It seems that we have an appetite for such tales, for

there are no fewer than three about boys who vanished while fetching water from the family well.

Sixteen-year-old Charles Ashmore of Illinois in November 1878, eleven-year-old Oliver Larch of Indiana on Christmas Eve 1889, and eleven-year-old Oliver Thomas of Rhayader, Wales, on Christmas Eve 1909, are all said to have made fateful trips across snow-covered yards. Footsteps showed plainly up to the well, but then, so the stories go, they ceased – and the boys were never seen again.

These tales make good scary stories for Christmas Eve – it's not likely that any eleven-year-old will volunteer to go outside afterwards – but probably that's all there is to them. There's no real need to worry that a 'black hole' may lurk in the fields, or lie in wait at the bottom of the garden.

16

Lizzie Borden and the Axe Murders

Lizzie Borden took an axe,
And gave her mother forty whacks.
When she saw what she had done,
She gave her father forty-one.

The rhyme doesn't get it quite right, though the truth was horrific enough. Abby Borden, who as Lizzie would have insisted was really her stepmother, was killed by nineteen blows, and her husband, Andrew, by eleven.

Moreover, the jury at Lizzie's trial decided that she didn't do it at all.

The murders, on 4 August 1892 at Fall River in Massachusetts, and the trial afterwards, gripped America and have fascinated people ever since. Was Lizzie truly innocent or did she, a Sunday school teacher with a butter-wouldn't-melt-in-my-mouth look, have the jury fooled?

Lizzie's real mother died when she was two, and she and her elder sister, Emma, never got on with their stepmother, though she was not unkind to them. By the time Lizzie was thirty-two, unmarried and still living at home, the bad feeling was worse.

Andrew Borden, whom Lizzie loved, was a wealthy property investor, yet they all lived in a cramped little house, where the rooms opened into each other and there was no privacy. They had an Irish girl, Bridget Sullivan, as their maid, and at the time of the murders Abby's brother John was staying with them. But Emma was away on holiday.

It was a very hot day. After breakfast the two men went out, while Abby, feather duster in hand, told Bridget to clean all the windows on the outside. Bridget was feeling sick, as Abby knew, and wasn't very happy with the order.

It was around nine o'clock when Abby made her fatal last journey upstairs to the guest-room. Lizzie was in her own room then – yet she claimed to have heard nothing when Abby was hacked to death in the room next door.

When Andrew came home about an hour and a half later, he went into the sitting-room with his newspaper, and must have dozed off on the settee. While asleep he was attacked with the same ferocity that destroyed his wife.

The sick Bridget was lying down to rest when, a little later, she heard Lizzie screaming that her father was dead. In the flurry that followed, with doctor, police and friends pouring into the house, it was some time before anyone looked for Abby.

When questioned about her morning Lizzie made contradictory statements and soon came under suspicion (though quite reasonably she said that with all the questions 'I am so confused that I don't know one thing from another').

The police knew that if Lizzie had killed her parents, she and her clothes must have been covered in blood. Yet she was as clean and well-dressed as usual, and though they searched for a dress she might have worn earlier they couldn't find one.

They did find a possible murder weapon: an axe-head, recently broken from its handle which was missing. Blood could have been washed from metal, but not from wood. Lizzie openly admitted that she had put 'one stick' into the stove that very hot morning.

Two days later the stove fire featured again. A friend found Lizzie thrusting 'an old dress' into it. It was, said Lizzie, stained with brown paint and not fit to wear again. The friend was deeply disturbed and told the court at the trial about the incident, but Emma supported her sister's story of the paint.

If Lizzie wasn't the murderer, who could have been? The police would have liked to pin the blame on rough-looking Uncle John, but luckily for him he had a cast-iron alibi, at least for Andrew's death. They also questioned Bridget very closely: she could have done it, but resentment at having to clean windows on a hot day didn't provide much of a motive.

The only other possibility was that some enemy of Andrew's got into the locked house unseen and unheard. He butchered Abby with an axe, then hid for two hours before killing Andrew and escaping, blood-stained but still unnoticed. It didn't seem very likely.

At her trial the jury saw Lizzie, demure, wide-eyed and accompanied daily to court by her church minister. They clearly found it impossible to imagine her wielding an axe in a frenzy. Nor could they believe that a daughter would kill the father she loved.

They were never told that Lizzie sometimes had 'funny spells' when she didn't seem to know what she was doing. No one suggested that a daughter might kill her loved father so that he would never know what she had done to his hated wife.

Lizzie was surely lucky to be found innocent. After her triumph she went back to Fall River and bought a new house where she lived, warily regarded by her neighbours, till 1927.

17

The Dogon Enigma

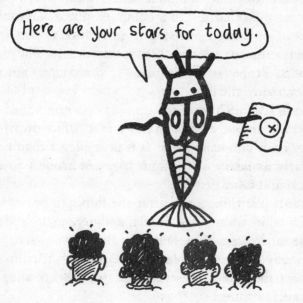

Here are your stars for today.

Is there life in outer space? Our sun is just one of 200,000 million stars in our own galaxy, and scientists estimate that there are 100 billion galaxies in the universe. So we can be sure that life-forms like our own exist elsewhere, even if we have never had direct knowledge of them. Or have we?

In Mali in Africa there is a tribe, the Dogons, who

have extraordinary knowledge of the heavens, and in particular of the brightest star in the sky, Sirius, the dog-star. This information came to astronomers only within the last hundred years, yet the Dogons, living simple lives in caves and mud huts, appear to have known it for centuries. They claim that they learnt it from beings from another world.

Sirius is twice as large as our sun and twenty times as bright. In 1844 an astronomer noted that Sirius's movements were irregular, and he deduced that the only explanation must be that it had a companion star, invisible to the naked eye, but exercising a gravitational pull on it. Nearly twenty years later a tiny speck of light was identified by telescope as the dog-star's companion, Sirius B, and nicknamed the Pup.

It wasn't till 1970 that the Pup was photographed, but by then astronomers knew that it was a 'white dwarf', an exceptionally condensed star. It is little bigger than Earth, yet nearly as heavy as the sun. Its orbit around Sirius is elliptical and takes fifty years.

In 1931, just three years after the Pup had been identified as a white dwarf, two French anthropologists, Marcel Griaule and Germaine Dieterlen, began to study the Dogon way of life. They earned the people's trust to such an extent that their priests agreed to reveal to them the tribe's secret beliefs.

They discovered that the star Sirius was important to the Dogons, but in itself that was not surprising. Sirius is so bright that many peoples (like the ancient Egyptians) have used its movements as a guide to their farming year.

What did amaze Griaule and Dieterlen was that the Dogons also spoke of Sirius's invisible companion, apparently knowing those things which astronomers had only just discovered: that it was white and very small, but very heavy. They drew the Pup's orbit around Sirius and correctly showed it as elliptical. They knew that it takes fifty years to orbit its bright companion.

They call the star 'Po Tolo', after the smallest object known to them – a tiny seed.

That is not the end of their astronomical knowledge, for without telescopes they are also aware that Saturn has rings, Jupiter four principal moons, and that the earth spins on its own axis.

How could they possibly know all this? They claim to have learnt it from the 'Nommos', whom they call the guardians of the universe. They say the Nommos came to them from a planet in the Sirius system – 8.6 light years away from us. They describe the apparent landing of a spacecraft, which came down 'spinning and whirling' with a noise like that of stones being struck in a cave.

They say these aliens were fish-like in appearance, 'masters of the water', and that their place of arrival was north-east of their present lands.

Some backing for this remarkable story comes from a study of other ancient cultures. In Babylonian mythology tales are told of strange beings, half fish, half man, called the Oannes, who are supposed to have come from the heavens in an egg-shaped vehicle and landed in the Red Sea. They were reputed to have taught men the principles of civilization.

Similar fish-bodied deities are found in Greek mythology, though not – as might be expected if these myths are based on reality – in ancient Egyptian.

Is there any way the Dogons could have learnt facts about Sirius in modern times and incorporated them into their culture? It has been pointed out that French schools were established in the Mali area in 1907, and that there is a Moslem university in Timbuktu, two hundred miles away. Maybe the tribesmen gained their knowledge from one of these sources.

But even if one can imagine a traveller both able to speak the Dogons' language and in possession of up-to-the-minute astronomical information, it doesn't seem a likely topic of conversation, and even less likely that the Dogon priests would immediately make it an essential part of their culture.

The Dogons also say that there is a third star with Sirius which is four times lighter than Po Tolo. No such star has yet been discovered, though in the 1920s some astronomers did think that they had found a Sirius C. This has since been disputed though not disproved. If it were to be found, it would be powerful confirmation of the very curious tale of the Dogons and their Nommos.

18

Wild Children

If you hatch a duck's egg yourself you will have to become mother duck too – the duckling will see you when it hatches and follow you everywhere. You'd better teach it to swim and grub for worms! Many cases have been recorded that seem to show that this so-called 'typing' can happen the other way round too, with wild animals adopting abandoned human children.

Until the great forests of Europe were swept away in

modern times, there were a number of reports of wolves apparently acting as guardians of children lost there, though it is odd that they should – against their reputation in fairy-tales!

The wolf-child of Hesse, for example, found naked in the forest in 1344, was believed to have lived under the protection of wolves for about four years. He could not speak, could not walk upright, and ate raw food. His captors attempted to 'humanize' him, fixing boards to his legs to force him to walk on two feet.

Nowadays such stories are more likely to come from Asia (where Kipling set his *Jungle Book* stories of Mowgli, who was adopted by wolves and educated by Baloo the bear). In 1973, for example, a boy was found in Sri Lanka in the company of monkeys, moving on all fours and making barking noises.

The wolf-children of Midnapore were found in 1920,

curled up in a ball with young wolves, after the mother wolf had been shot. The two girls, aged about three and eight, were thought not to be sisters. How had they come to be there? Could the mother wolf originally have intended them for food for her babies?

They were taken to an orphanage, and named Amala (Bright Yellow Flower) and Kamala (Lotus). But they were not at all flower-like! They snarled and growled at humans, baring their teeth. They would eat only raw meat, gulping it down like dogs. Photos show Kamala eating and drinking on the ground like an animal. She used her hands like paws and could run very fast on all fours.

The girls were night creatures, never sleeping after midnight. When they did sleep it was on top of each other like puppies, and with knees up to their chests, even when lying on their backs.

Unhappily though, both girls died at the orphanage. Kamala did live long enough to learn to walk upright, eat food normally, and speak a few words, but she never lost all her animal habits.

The sad thing about these real-life Mowglis is that taking them from the wild rarely helps them. Unlike Mowgli they seem unable to readapt to human life and, like Amala and Kamala, usually die young.

Some people dispute that these children have been brought up by animals at all. They suggest that the children fail to pick up human ways because they are mentally abnormal, cruelly abandoned by their parents for that reason, and that the animal connection is just made-up fantasy.

But others argue that the children couldn't have survived in the wild at all if they hadn't had their wits about them. How the child/animal partnership comes about is impossible to explain, but there is more to it than just finding a child in the company of animals.

They often develop special characteristics – such as the velvety skin of the Midnapore girls, who didn't seem to feel the cold. They have very acute hearing and sense of smell and can see in the dark. Smiling is a human form of communication, learned from a mother, and these children do not laugh or smile.

The 'gazelle-boy' of the Sahara was so much a part of the herd that he leapt about, twitched his ears and scalp at any suspicion of danger, and joined in the herd's rituals of sniffing.

He was found and observed in 1946 by the French anthropologist, Jean-Claude Armen, who watched and recorded his behaviour, but perhaps wisely left him where he was.

The gazelle-boy, aged about ten, existed happily on a diet of roots. Others of these wild children have been recorded eating bark, grass, and even hay, so the human stomach is clearly more adaptable than we think, at least in childhood.

Wild children are still being found – as recently as 1985 a wolf-boy known as Ramu died in Mother Teresa's Home for the Destitute in Lucknow in India. He'd been discovered in the company of three wolves, and his hands were calloused from walking on all fours. He would attack chickens and devour the flesh raw!

While it is difficult to see what sort of life these children could have grown up to, their early deaths in what to them was captivity suggest that well-meaning adults should think hard before taking them from the wild. Given a choice probably all the children would have opted for the jungle or forest and the companionship of animals.

19

The Death of
William the Red

Just off the A31 near Minstead in the New Forest stands
the Rufus Stone, marking the spot where William II, son
of the Conqueror, was killed in 1100. It also marks the
site of an ancient mystery – was William's an accidental
death, was he murdered, or, even more sinisterly, was he
a willing sacrificial victim of a pagan religion?

William was certainly no Christian, and was hated by
churchmen, largely for the way in which he seized church
money. They were ready after his death to see the hand
of God at work, and to imagine the hell flames which
must be gobbling him up.

William Rufus, nicknamed for his blazing red hair,
was a powerful king – 'the wind and the sea seemed to
obey him', wrote one man. He was strong physically, and

loved deer-hunting in the New Forest. On 2 August 1100, he went for his last, fatal, hunt.

It is said that all kinds of ominous events preceded it. The Devil was reputed to be abroad in the Forest. William himself is supposed to have woken from a frightful nightmare that morning, in which he saw his own blood stream up to the heavens and block out the light.

Monks are said to have brought reports of dreams in which William was consigned to hell. These he dismissed saying that monks were a 'parcel of wheezing old women'.

But, old women's words or not, William delayed setting out hunting. Normally he would have set off first thing. Had he been affected after all by these dreams?

Late in the day the hunting party did ride off. Accompanying the king were his younger brother Henry, a number of English lords, and Walter Tyrel, a French nobleman who was his guest. The party dismounted and fanned out, ready with bows and arrows to shoot at the deer which would be driven past.

Precisely what happened next is unclear – there are various versions – but it seems that as the sun was setting the king was alone in a glade with Tyrel when a stag crossed in front of him. The king let fly but did not bring it down. Shielding his eyes from the sun he watched it run on.

Tyrel then loosed an arrow, but unintentionally struck the king (some reports say the shot was deflected from a tree). William made no sound, but breaking off the shaft from the arrow-head in his chest fell on it, thus hastening his death.

Tyrel didn't wait, but leaping on his horse rode for the coast and a ship to France. Nor did anyone else aid the stricken king. Henry galloped to nearby Winchester to secure the throne for himself (William had no children). The other nobles all raced away too, perhaps in panic.

It was left to a peasant to load William's body on to a cart and take it, profusely bleeding, to Winchester for burial. The service which was held next day was noticeably brief and without even the normal tolling of bells.

This lack of ceremony, added to Henry's apparent heartlessness when his brother fell and his failure to make any public inquiry into the shooting, have roused suspicion that William's death was pre-arranged. Others justify Henry's race to Winchester in that there was another brother who would also claim the throne.

Walter Tyrel later denied responsibility for any crime. Those who think Henry staged a hunting 'accident' suggest that Tyrel was made scapegoat because he was a foreigner – but had that been the plan, Henry would surely have held an inquiry to pin the blame officially on him. Tyrel may just have meant that he hadn't intended William's death.

What of the suggestion that William's death was a pagan sacrifice? It was made by an anthropologist, Margaret Murray, who thought that the 'old' religion still held sway in England long after Christianity became the official religion.

In pagan times there was a belief that a god-king had to be sacrificed to ensure the fertility of crops and animals. Murray noted that William died at a time known as Lammas, which had been important in the pagan calendar.

She believed that William had ordered Tyrel to shoot him (one version of the death, written some time afterwards, has William shouting to him 'Draw, draw your

74

bow for the Devil's sake, and let your arrow fly or it will be the worse for you'). She thinks William fell on the arrow deliberately.

So he may – he was a brave man, and may have wanted to avoid a lingering death. Interesting though it is, there isn't enough evidence to make Murray's theory convincing.

Few people, even at the time, knew the exact circumstances of William the Red's death, but the sudden shock of it produced many legends. It is still said that on the anniversary of his death William's ghost follows the route that his corpse took, dripping blood.

20

The Everest Mystery

When George Mallory was asked why he wanted to climb Everest, he is supposed to have replied, 'Because it's there'. Reaching the summit of the highest mountain in the world is still many climbers' ambition. But since Sir Edmund Hillary and Sherpa Tenzing set foot on its peak in 1953, the struggle to be first on the top is over.

Were they really the first though? The question which hangs over mountaineering history is, did the tragedy of George Mallory's death, and that of his companion Sandy Irvine, follow the triumph of being first men on the top?

It was in 1852 that a peak in the Himalayas was measured by British surveyors at over 8,840 metres, and recognized as the highest mountain on earth. Nobody knew

the Tibetan name for it – Chomolungma, Goddess Mother of the World – and so it was named Everest after Sir George Everest, the chief surveyor.

At first no one thought of climbing it, but by the 1920s the British, having missed being first to the South Pole, were determined to make the conquest of Everest a British affair.

Everest sets climbers two main problems: climate and altitude. Vicious storms sweep the mountainside, the freezing temperatures can cause frost-bite, and the rarefied atmosphere makes every step a breathless effort.

In those days climbers were ill-equipped to deal with either problem. They went up Everest looking as if on a country walk, in tweed jackets, mufflers, and felt hats. Oxygen cylinders, available to help overcome the problems of thin air, were heavy and unreliable, and some people thought it was cheating to use them.

In 1924 George Mallory, a brilliant rock-climber who had been on Everest before, was made climbing leader of a new expedition. Aged thirty-seven, Mallory knew that this would be his last chance to get to the top, and he wanted to try with oxygen.

He chose Andrew (Sandy) Irvine to be his partner in the summit attempt. Irvine was only twenty-two, with little climbing experience, but he was strong, brave, and a wizard with the awkward cylinders.

The planned route was up the north-east ridge of the mountain, using an established series of camps. The starting point was Camp III and they set out on 6 June.

By the following evening they had reached Camp VI, at around 8,200 metres. It was a single tent, bleak and cheerless. At such an altitude water boils when it is lukewarm, so they wouldn't even have been able to make a hot drink. From there, on the morning of 8 June, they struck out for the summit.

Climbing up behind Mallory and Irvine that day, to meet them on return to Camp VI, was Noel Odell, the expedition's geologist.

Odell was jubilant as he explored the rocks and discovered the first fossils on Everest. Cloud was round him, but at mid-morning it lifted briefly and the whole summit was revealed. Suddenly his eyes fixed on 'one tiny black spot silhouetted on a small snow-crest beneath a rock-step on the ridge'.

Then the black spot moved and was joined by another. After a few minutes the spots appeared at the top of the step. It could only have been Mallory and Irvine 'going strong for the top'. Then the cloud closed in and the figures were lost from sight.

Odell waited for his friends till late afternoon, but then, because Camp VI could only accommodate two men, he went back down to Camp IV. Two days later he climbed up to Camp VI again, to find his worst fears realized. Mallory and Irvine had not come back. They must have fallen, or been overtaken by night and frozen to death on the bare mountain.

Could they have reached the summit before disaster struck? When Odell saw them they were behind schedule. Even so, he felt that they could have got to the top by four o'clock.

But in 1933 the next Everest expedition concluded that the so-called 'second step' of the ridge, on the top of which Odell believed he'd seen the two men, could not be climbed. (They also found an ice-axe below the first step, which probably marked the spot where one or both climbers had slipped.)

In 1985, however, a Spanish team reached the summit by a route which included the 'impossible' second step. They felt that Mallory and Irvine could have got to the top, but would not have been able to get back to Camp VI before night.

Perhaps one day we shall know. In 1986, believing that the bodies of Mallory and Irvine must still lie somewhere on the mountain, an expedition set out to try to recover them – and their camera. But thwarted by deep snow, they found nothing.

If the camera is ever recovered and the film can be processed, most will surely hope that it will show that before their deaths Mallory and Irvine did achieve a moment of glory.

21

The Skidding Stones of Racetrack Playa

In lane one...Rocky Boulder...

Death Valley, high in the Sierra Nevada mountains of California, is not a comfortable place to be. As the name suggests men have died here, lost while gold prospecting in the barren hills.

Yet tourists drive for miles, bumping over the dirt road past Jackass Spring, Hidden Valley and Tea Kettle Junction, to reach Racetrack Playa and see its strange phenomenon: stones which seem to move by themselves.

Playas are flat, dried-up beds of what once were lakes. Occasional thunderstorms flood the ground a centimetre or so, but mainly the sun scorches down on to cracked, parched earth.

Stones large and small lie scattered over the three-mile-long Racetrack Playa, but the odd thing is that many look as if they have indeed entered for races. Each appears at the end of a furrowed track as if driven across the ground and skidding to a stop.

Some of the tracks are lengthy. One hefty 320-kilogram rock left behind it a trail of 174 metres. Smaller stones have made journeys of over a mile. Sometimes the trails are straight, sometimes curved, sometimes they zig-zag to and fro or criss-cross each other's tracks. Lively little stones appear to have tumbled or somersaulted as they shot across the level ground.

The slipping and sliding seems to take place only at night, and no one has ever witnessed a stone in motion.

Landslides and earthquakes apart, we don't expect stones to move. We'd be very surprised if we looked out of a window and saw that the garden rockery had gone walkabout. So what explanation can be offered for these extraordinary movements? It's a problem that fascinates scientists.

Could it all be a human hoax? Investigators have tried pushing and pulling stones across the Playa, but the furrows they made were much deeper than the natural ones. In any case, Racetrack Playa is too difficult to get at and too uncomfortable to be in, for hoaxers to stick at it year after year.

It has been argued that the stones move in winter when thin ice sheets form. Stones embedded in ice could be blown with it by the strong winds which funnel through the mountains.

But two American geologists, Robert F. Sharp and

Dwight L. Carey, think differently. In the 1970s they set themselves to study the stones systematically. They chose twenty-five of various shapes and sizes, marked them, gave them all girls' names, and waited to see if Mary Ann, Ruth, Sue, Sally, Val and company would move. They did!

During seven years of record-keeping, almost all the marked stones set off on at least one journey. Some became seasoned travellers. Lightweight Nancy (250 grams) travelled furthest in one go – 201 metres – but even the heavy Dottie (24.3 kilograms) managed sixty-one metres (once was enough for her though).

The scientists were sure that ice did not cause the travelling. In one experiment they used metal rods to stake out a corral for two unchristened stones: one escaped, leaving its companion behind, which would be impossible if a sliding sheet of ice was responsible.

Instead they concluded that wind and rain are the decisive factors. After rain the Playa surface turns to a thin, greasy layer of mud. At such times they think that strong gusts of wind catch the stones and set them sailing across the slippery surface.

The two men noted that the stones moved after winter storms, and mainly in the direction of the prevailing north-easterly wind. Oddly though, the marks left by the stone called Kirsty showed that she'd set off north then abruptly changed her mind and come shooting back again, finishing up not far from her starting point.

Sharp and Carey must surely have got near the truth, though a few doubts have been expressed. Could wind ever be strong enough to shift the really heavy stones? Why, when stones are in a group together, do some move off while others stay still?

Perhaps one day the TV cameras will be there to record the movements, and we shall see the slipping, sliding stones set off on their jaunts.

22

The Man in the Iron Mask

In 1703 a man who had been a prisoner for thirty-four years died in the Bastille, the great French fortress prison, and was buried at night in great secrecy and under a false name.

In his long years as prisoner of King Louis XIV his true identity had been totally erased. He was never known by name, and was on pain of instant death forbidden to speak of himself. His whole face was concealed by a mask. (It was not actually an iron one as later legend suggested, but made of black velvet, probably with a metal hinge to allow him to open his mouth.)

He was always under the command of the same prison governor, and when the governor moved, so did his prisoner. In each new gaol thousands of pounds were spent on creating a secure cell for him, with triple doors and many-barred windows.

Yet within this secure cell the king allowed his prisoner to live in style. He could have whatever he wanted and even dined off silver plates.

Who was he? What terrible crime had he committed or what secret knowledge did he possess that he must be silenced so? And why, if his existence posed such a threat to the king, was he not simply killed?

These are questions which people began to ask as rumours of the nameless prisoner circulated, and three hundred years later they still cannot be answered with complete certainty.

Alexandre Dumas in the last of his musketeer novels, *The Man in the Iron Mask*, suggested that he was the older twin brother of Louis XIV and therefore the rightful king. This was an attractive theory, except that it would have been quite impossible for Queen Anne, Louis's mother, to conceal the birth of twins. And why should she? Two heirs are better than one.

There have been many guesses as to the mysterious prisoner's identity, from an illegitimate son of the English King Charles II, to an Italian diplomat who foolishly tried to swindle Louis XIV.

But in 1890 a historian's careful study of letters to the prison governor showed that the masked man had first reached gaol in 1669 as 'Eustache Dauger', arrested in Dunkirk.

The next question was, who was Eustache Dauger? Was that his real name, or one made up to disguise his true identity? In the 1930s more historical detective work by a French historian suggested the answer.

There had been a large and successful family named Cavoye. The father, François, was until his death captain of the musketeers. His elder sons were unfortunately killed in battle and a younger son became the family heir. His name was Eustache, and his full name was Eustache d'Auger de Cavoye.

As a boy, one year older than Louis XIV, he had been one of the future king's companions. But in 1668 Eustache was involved in a scandal and stripped of his rights of inheritance. In 1669 he disappeared from history completely, just at the time when Eustache Dauger was arrested.

It seems certain that the two men were the same, the name slightly disguised, and soon to be dropped from all records.

So, what had he done, and was his being in Dunkirk significant? It has been suggested both that he was trying to escape from France and that he was coming back from some failed secret mission to England.

It is unlikely that we shall ever know for sure the terrible knowledge that Eustache took with him to the grave, but there has been one very interesting guess.

What would we have seen if we had been able to look beneath the mask? Could it have been a face much resembling that of the most important figure in the country: the king?

No portrait of Eustache exists, but his brother Louis, who was one of Louis XIV's close associates, was said to be remarkably like his royal friend, as a portrait of him shows.

Suppose they were half-brothers? When Louis XIV was born it seemed little short of a miracle to the French people. Louis XIII and his queen had been married for twenty-two years without children. All were worried about what would happen if the king died without an heir. Then in rapid succession Queen Anne gave birth to two princes – Louis and Philippe. Could François de Cavoye, the loyal musketeer, have been their real father?

If this was the secret which Eustache discovered then it would have meant that Louis had no right to the throne of France. If Eustache was Louis's half-brother and knew it (perhaps even trying to blackmail the king?) he would have had to be silenced. But Louis might have hesitated to kill his one-time friend.

Perhaps Alexandre Dumas was not very far from the truth after all.

23

The Empty Lighthouse

Though three men dwell on Flannan Isle
To keep the lamp alight,
As we steer'd under the lee we caught
No glimmer through the night!

This is the beginning of W. W. Gibson's poem 'Flannan Isle', about the real-life mystery of an empty lighthouse.

The story of the empty lighthouse...
Is there anything in it?

The Flannan Islands lie west of the Hebrides, and in past centuries ships sailing up or down the Scottish coast were often wrecked on the lonely, rocky islands. So in 1895 it was decided to build a lighthouse on the one known as Eilean Mor (meaning 'Big Island'). Turbulent seas made it difficult to land building materials, so it was four years before, in December 1899, the warning light shone out for the first time.

A year later three keepers, Thomas Marshall, James Ducat and Donald McArthur, were serving shifts on the island. A relief keeper, Joseph Moore, was due to be landed with supplies just before Christmas, but because of bad weather the steamer, the *Hesperus*, was not able to sail till 26 December.

As the *Hesperus* approached Eilean Mor the men on

board expected to see a signal flag go up to show that they had been spotted. But there was no response. The ship's horn was sounded and a rocket fired, but no one came hurrying to the quay. The captain ordered Moore to land and investigate.

Nervous of what he might find Moore made his way up to the lighthouse. The entrance gate was shut and the outer door too. Inside, the kitchen door was open and he entered and looked around. Ashes lay cold in the fireplace and the clocks had stopped. Otherwise all was in order, beds made, dishes washed from the last meal. But of the men there was no sign.

The *Hesperus* was forced to return to the mainland and report the unexplained loss of all three keepers. Moore was left behind with three volunteers to man the light, and next day they conducted a thorough search of the island. They found nothing, apart from storm damage to one of the jetties.

What could have happened? At first, it was assumed that all three men must have lost their lives in an accident during the recent storms. A last entry on the log-slate was for 1 p.m. on 15 December. That this was the day when disaster struck was confirmed by a steamer captain who had sailed past the island that night but had seen no light.

Two sets of oilskins were missing and it was conjectured that two men had gone to the quay, perhaps to rescue or secure storm-damaged equipment, and had fallen or been dragged by a wave into the sea. The third man, going to the rescue, had somehow suffered catastrophe too.

Then it was realized that on 15 December the seas had been calm and the storms had not yet begun.

The log entries, made by Thomas Marshall, proved

peculiar. He reported a great gale raging on 12 December, with seas 'tearing' at the lighthouse. Yet on the Island of Lewis, only twenty miles away, there had been no storm.

Marshall mentions Ducat being 'irritable', McArthur 'crying', and all of them praying. The last entry on 15 December reads 'Storm ended, sea calm, God is over all'. Had one of the keepers gone mad, suffering a storm in the mind, and brought about the deaths by drowning of all three? It's a possibility, though the lack of any disorder argues against the theory.

A different explanation was offered in 1947 by a Scottish journalist, Iain Campbell. Visiting Eilean Mor on a day of calm, he was startled when the quiet-seeming sea gave a sudden heave and rose the full twenty metres up and over the jetty. He thought that the men might have been caught and swept away by a similar freak surge. But why were all three on the quay at once, one of them in shirt-sleeves?

There is another idea. Archie Lamont, the father of a friend of mine, was one of the *Hesperus* men who volunteered to stay and help the agitated Moore keep the lighthouse going. He used to suggest that the men had 'done a bunk': that is, arranged to be picked up by a passing steamer and taken off to Australia or New Zealand to start new lives.

But though one man might have wanted to disappear, it's hard to believe that all three would want to leave home. In any case, my friend thinks that deep down, as a superstitious Highlander, her father believed that something uncanny had occurred.

W. W. Gibson in his poem writes of 'three queer, black, ugly birds' seen on the island after the men's disappearance, hinting that they might have been transformed. Probably it was only the product of his distressed mind, but Moore afterwards thought that amongst the cries of the sea-birds he could hear the voices of his former companions calling.

If Eilean Mor is a place of ghosts, however, today there is no one there to see or hear. Since 1971 the lighthouse has run automatically, being visited only now and again for maintenance.

24

The Great Pyramid

'Man fears time, but time fears the pyramids', runs an old Arab saying. They have stood in the Egyptian desert for 5,000 years, plundered for centuries for their stone, yet still among the most impressive monuments on earth.

The finest and biggest of all, named centuries ago as

one of the Seven Wonders of the World, is the Great Pyramid of Cheops. But it is so massive, and built with such mathematical precision, that it has always been a puzzle as to how a society with only primitive building tools could have created it.

Cheops became ruler of Egypt in 2550 BC, and probably began construction of the pyramid that was to be his tomb at once.

For the Ancient Egyptians life after death was more important than life on earth, especially for Pharaohs. They chose burial in pyramids because a pyramid's shape imitated the spread of the sun's rays, up which the Pharaoh's soul would rise to be united with the sun-god Ra.

No pyramid was grander in design than Cheops'. It covers about thirteen acres: it is said that you could fit five of the greatest cathedrals in Europe into its base, and a few houses too.

Despite its huge scale there is less than twenty centimetres of difference between the lengths of its 230-metre sides. Moreover, the angle at which the sides rise is equally accurate. As if that wasn't enough, the whole pyramid is exactly aligned north, south, east and west. This shows that the builders had sophisticated understanding of the stars.

It's been estimated that some 2,300,000 limestone blocks went into its construction, each weighing between two and a half and fifteen tons, and so accurately cut that the gaps between can only be measured in millimetres.

How did they do it? Without cranes, bulldozers, lorries, sophisticated cutting equipment and mathematical instruments?

There are those who can't believe that they did. The

pyramidiots, as archaeologists call them, suggest other-worldly builders: aliens from other planets, or the hand of God.

But if we assume that the Egyptians knew what they were doing, having the kind of skills which develop over generations, then we might suggest that first they flooded the base area to see what humps and bumps needed levelling. Once the base was accurately marked out, building could begin.

The limestone used for the bulk of the pyramid was quarried nearby, dragged on sledges and then probably up ramps of mud and chippings, rising as the pyramid grew. Smooth facing-stone (almost all now lost) was quarried from the other side of the Nile, and must have been ferried over on boats. These facing-stones would have been put in place from the top downwards, the ramps gradually being removed, till the whole pyramid was revealed, brilliantly reflecting the desert sunlight.

If it was finished by the end of Cheops' twenty-three-year reign, then 100,000 blocks would have had to be put in place every year. Masons could have worked year round in the quarry preparing the stone, but the arduous job of dragging the blocks into position would probably only have taken place in summer when the Nile flooded and farming was impossible.

When the Pharaoh died, his mummified body would have been placed inside a sarcophagus within the pyramid. But here is another mystery: what has happened to the corpse, for which all this grandeur was prepared? None has been found.

No pyramid has a door. They were designed to frustrate would-be tomb robbers. But in AD 820 an Arab ruler sent his men to force a way in, in search of treasure.

After excavating an entrance they found themselves breaking into a downward-sloping passage. It led to an empty cavity. Then a stone falling from the roof showed that there was another upwards passage, though it was hidden by tight-fitting granite plugs which blocked the opening and which must have been fitted from above.

They cut their way round and found themselves going up, first to another empty chamber, then, through a lofty gallery, to a final grand chamber. But the granite coffin within was empty.

What had happened? Could priests have removed the body and its accompanying treasures some time after the funeral, using the shaft which provided an escape route for those who sealed up the passage? It would have been a tricky operation. But robbers wouldn't have bothered about concealing the openings afterwards.

Perhaps Cheops was never buried in his pyramid at all? But if not, why go to the trouble of sealing the ascending corridor?

Was it all a blind? Is it possible that Cheops is still somewhere in his enormous pyramid? In 1987 archaeologists used sound-sensing equipment to look for any hidden chamber. However, though they did find unknown cavities they could detect no large spaces. Even so, it remains possible that the Great Pyramid hasn't revealed all its secrets yet.

25

The Bermuda Triangle

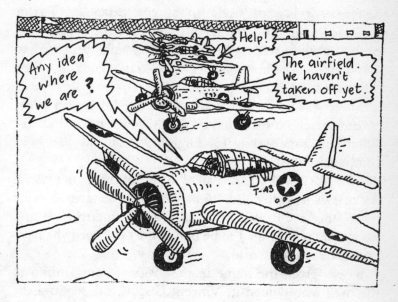

At 2 p.m. on 5 December 1945, five Avenger torpedo bombers set off from Fort Lauderdale in Florida for a routine-practice bombing and navigation exercise. The flight, which was given the number nineteen, was led by a young lieutenant, Charles Taylor. At first all went well, but an hour and forty minutes into their mission Taylor was in trouble.

He radioed that both his compasses were out and he did not know where he was. He could see land and thought he was over the chain of little islands called the Florida Keys, so he was given instructions for navigating visually from there.

It is likely, however, that the planes were over the northern Bahamas, islands which look much like the Keys. In that case the directions Taylor received would have led them even further astray.

By early evening Flight 19 was still lost, and running dangerously low on fuel. In the emergency Lt. Taylor remained calm and courageous. He gave the order to all planes to close into tight formation and be prepared to ditch: 'When the first plane drops to ten gallons we all go down together.'

There was no further radio contact and despite a widespread search no survivors or wreckage were ever located. What had gone wrong for Flight 19, and why had both compasses failed?

This story of the 'Lost Patrol' is one of the main mysteries of the so-called Bermuda Triangle, an area formed when lines are drawn between Florida, Puerto Rico and Bermuda, and claimed to be one of the most eerily hazardous waters in the world.

It was given the name in the 1960s, but according to the man who coined it, Vincent Gaddis, the sea and the sky have for centuries been the 'scene of disappearances that total far beyond the laws of chance'.

Certainly, strange things have been recorded as happening to ships and planes in the area. Just after dawn in April 1955, for example, a ball of fire passed above a merchant vessel called the *Atlantic City*. The ship, which was on automatic steering, started going round in a circle and the compass equipment failed completely.

In another weird incident in 1966 the *Good News*, a tug on a voyage from Puerto Rico to Fort Lauderdale, found itself enveloped in thick, milky fog, the compass needle spinning wildly and all electric power lost. The sea was turbulent and at full steam ahead the ship only just managed to make headway. When clear of the fog the captain discovered to his amazement that the bad weather was only local: the sea around was calm and visibility good.

Even the QE2 had trouble with unaccountable electrical and mechanical failure on a voyage in 1974. At the same time its radar image disappeared from a nearby coastguard vessel.

Missionaries Warren and Betty Miller had a hair-raising time in 1975 *en route* to Florida in a light aircraft. They flew into a 'yellowish haze', their instruments failed, and for two hours they circled hopelessly until, emerging from the mist, their radio and equipment functioned again.

Such stories suggest that navigational equipment may be affected by fluctuations of the earth's magnetic field, and indeed tests carried out from space have shown it to be very variable. It has been suggested that movements within the earth's molten iron core where magnetic forces are generated may cause a sudden 'magnetic earthquake', producing the compass distortions and instrument failures noted in the Bermuda Triangle.

On the other hand, the Triangle's evil reputation has been disputed. Bearing in mind that these are seas of sudden and severe storms, the recorded losses of ships and planes are not strikingly more dramatic than anywhere else.

Moreover, investigators have found that some of the so-called mysterious shipwrecks can easily be explained in terms of weather, human failure, or unseaworthiness.

Even the disappearance of Flight 19 can be accounted for. If Taylor believed that his compasses had failed only because he thought he knew where he was, then the tragic loss of fourteen young men is explicable just as human error.

Yet the tales of survivors of disturbing experiences in the Triangle do suggest that out-of-the-ordinary ship and plane losses may have occurred. Moreover, the Triangle is capable of throwing up other, different, mysteries.

In 1991 there was great excitement when a group of divers announced that they had discovered Flight 19 on the sea-bed off Florida. But a couple of days later they had to admit that these five planes were not the Lost Patrol. Instead they formed a group which no one had ever reported missing!

26

Was Napoleon Murdered?

In the summer of 1821 the news reached Europe that Napoleon, great hero or villain according to your point of view, was dead. Thousands wept, thousands rejoiced: but one man may have gloated with silent satisfaction.

A strong case has been made in recent years that Napoleon did not die of natural causes but had been murdered.

When the French Emperor was defeated by Wellington at the Battle of Waterloo in 1815, the British were determined that he would never again be able to raise an army. They sent him into exile on the British-garrisoned island of St Helena in the south Atlantic, 4,000 miles away.

He was allowed to take with him a small band of followers, and at first life was not too bad. He lodged with the Balcombes, an English family, and made friends with the fourteen-year-old daughter, Betsey. To him she was 'Mademoiselle Betsee', and he let her call him 'Boney' and tease him.

But when he moved to Longwood House, prepared for him by the English, the daily routine became very dreary and restricted. Napoleon began to feel ill and accused the English of trying to bring about his death. After six dismal years and much suffering he died on 5 May 1821, aged fifty-one.

Though there has always been argument about the exact cause of death, no one suspected murder until 1955 when a Swedish dentist, Sten Forshufvud, read the account of Napoleon's last days by Louis Marchaud, his valet.

Forshufvud was a man not only fascinated by the history of Napoleon, but also by the scientific study of poisons. As he read, he realized that Napoleon's symptoms could have been caused by acute arsenic poisoning.

This form of poisoning was favoured by murderers in the past because the symptoms could be confused with genuine illnesses. Arsenic has no smell and is virtually tasteless so was not easy to detect in food or drink. If given to the victim a little at a time, suspicion of foul play was unlikely.

Forshufvud felt he knew what had happened to Napoleon but didn't see how he could prove it without studying his body. That was in Paris, under thirty-five tons of immovable marble!

Then in 1959, the Swede heard of a Scottish scientist, Hamilton Smith, who had invented a way of discovering arsenic in human hair: the body uses hair growth as a way of expelling the poison. If Forshufvud could get just one hair from Napoleon it could be tested.

He knew that after death Marchaud shaved his master's head and distributed the hair in the fashion of the time to his admirers. The Swede managed to find a Frenchman who had inherited some of this hair, and who gave him just one strand.

Hamilton Smith tested it and found it contained thirteen times more arsenic than would be normal!

Forshufvud was jubilant, but knew that to make an acceptable case he must test more hairs. It took him several years to acquire enough but in the end he did, including hair given originally to Betsey Balcombe. These samples showed that the Emperor had been absorbing large amounts of arsenic from the time he left the Balcombes' house.

Who could have been the traitor? It had to be someone who had been with Napoleon all six years (it couldn't be the English as they had no access to his food). Of the very few suspects by far the most likely candidate for murderer was the Count de Montholon, the man in charge of the Emperor's wine supply. Napoleon always drank wine from his own bottle, so arsenic slipped into it would not be drunk by anyone else.

Unlike Marchaud, Montholon had no record of loyal devotion to Napoleon before his exile, and as an aristocrat his sympathies might be expected to be with the newly-restored kings of France. If he did poison Napoleon he may well have done so on the orders of the Count d'Artois, heir to the throne. For many years d'Artois had been Napoleon's most fanatical enemy, and he had schemed to assassinate him several times.

But was there really such a plot? No poisoner would want to draw attention to himself with a sudden death, but to drag it out over six years seems equally dangerous. Is there any other way the arsenic could have got into his body?

In 1982 Dr David Jones showed that the wallpaper in Longwood House contained arsenic (it was used then as a colouring pigment). He suggested that was the source of the poison. However, unless Napoleon was in the habit of licking the walls it's difficult to see how he could have absorbed so much.

In his will Napoleon wrote: 'I die prematurely, murdered by the English oligarchy [group of rulers] and its hired assassin.' He was thinking of the English Governor of St Helena and making a political point. But if he had changed the words to 'French monarchy' he might possibly have been close to the truth.

27

The Siberian Disaster

Great natural disasters such as earthquakes and hurricanes usually claim many human victims. Yet when an extraterrestrial object exploded with the force of a nuclear bomb over the forests of Siberia, at 7.17 a.m. on 30 June 1908, not one human life was lost.

Because Siberia was so remote in those days, western scientists who recorded the shock waves that twice circled the earth afterwards did not know what had caused them, or the spectacular light effects which were seen worldwide. The most violent explosion in history was largely ignored.

It was not till thirteen years later that a Russian mineralogist, Leonid Kulik, grew interested in Siberian newspaper reports about what had happened in 1908. He became convinced that a large meteorite had crashed to earth there.

He read accounts of how people had seen a giant fireball 'brighter than the sun', how they had been thrown in the air by a great blast, had heard a thunderous explosion which rocked their houses, and had feared it was the end of the world. These people, he afterwards discovered, lived up to 200 miles from the centre of the blast.

Kulik got permission to travel to Siberia to investigate and to try to find the giant crater which he was sure would lie somewhere in Siberia's dark forests.

In 1927 he set out. Travel through the vast, uninhabited forests was extremely difficult. From the eyewitness accounts he knew the direction to take, but there were no roads or even paths, and he had to hack his way through dense undergrowth.

Finally he stood by a river and saw on the opposite bank that the ground had been stripped of its trees. The sight when he climbed a hill on the other side was awesome. Giant trees, 'snapped across like twigs', lay stretched to the horizon. The trunks all pointed in one direction, so Kulik knew that the centre of the devastation lay much further away.

Eventually he reached a 'great cauldron', an area a mile across, which he slowly circled to confirm that the fallen trees radiated out from it. He knew then that he had found the centre of the explosion.

Kulik made several expeditions but it was not until 1938 that the full extent of the damage was learned. Then aerial photos showed that 700 square miles of forest had been devastated.

But Kulik was wrong. Whatever flattened an area the size of a big city like Birmingham or Manchester, was not a meteorite. His giant cauldron was a natural formation, not an impact crater, and there were no chunks of the iron a meteorite would leave. But traces of cosmic dust showed that whatever had exploded had come from outer space. So what was it?

In 1946 a Russian scientist proposed a dramatic theory: than an alien spaceship, fuelled by nuclear power, had exploded. He pointed to the similarities between the Siberian event and the Hiroshima bomb of 1945. In both instances trees at the centre of the blast remained undamaged; afterwards plant growth was abnormally fast, and there was evidence of genetic change.

Eyewitness accounts of the path of the fire-ball varied and might be acceptable if a stricken spaceship had altered course, though nobody actually saw a change of direction.

Another popular idea has been that a black hole hit the earth. Black holes are said to occur when objects in space collapse in on themselves and form bodies so dense that light cannot escape from them. If a black hole no bigger than an atom (and representing what perhaps had been an asteroid of 100 kilometres across) were to enter our atmosphere, the explosive force created would be much like that experienced in Siberia.

The objection to this theory is that the black hole would afterwards have passed straight through the earth and created similar havoc when it emerged in the Atlantic, and there are no reports of great oceanic upheavals in 1908.

The most generally accepted explanation of the fireball is that it was a comet, or perhaps part of one which had broken away from a comet known to have circled the earth around that time.

The comet theory has been disputed because, with their long fiery tails, comets are usually easy to spot in the night sky, but nothing was seen of the 'flame which cut the sky in half' till just before it exploded.

However, it's been pointed out that not all comets have highly visible streamers, and that coming in on a path in line with the rising sun it would have been almost invisible.

One thing is certain: scientists say that sooner or later such an event will happen again. We were lucky last time – if the earth had been six hours further on in its orbit St Petersburg would probably have been wiped out – can we hope to get off so lightly next time?

28

The Money Pit

In the summer of 1795, a sixteen-year-old boy, Daniel McGinnis, set out in his canoe from his home in a small town on the coast of Nova Scotia in Canada. He paddled across to Oak Island, named for its covering of red oak trees.

Exploring the uninhabited island he came to a place where the trees had been cut down. One large central tree remained and Daniel noticed that one of its branches had been cut off and that the stump, apparently scored with rope marks, overhung a depression in the ground.

Next day Daniel returned with two friends. The boys were excited, believing that they'd located a pirate treasure hoard.

With picks and shovels they set about digging. A metre

First platform 3 metres down

down they came on a layer of flagstones. Three metres below that was a platform of oak logs, and another and another at three-metre intervals. They were certain now that treasure lay beneath them, but with their simple tools they could dig no deeper.

Back home they could find no one who would help them because the island was said to be haunted. Nine years passed before a group of treasure-hunters got together and digging resumed.

Down and down the men dug, as before finding oak platforms at regular intervals. They had been sealed with putty and coconut fibre. At twenty-seven metres they excavated a flat stone inscribed with a coded message, later deciphered as 'Ten feet below two million pounds'.

The earth was now waterlogged and they were bailing out twice as much water as earth. But one Saturday night, at thirty-metres depth, they probed and struck something which they were convinced was the wood of a chest. Victory seemed in sight but it was late and the sabbath at hand, so they went home.

In eager anticipation the men returned on Monday morning. But they faced disaster: the pit had flooded. Pumping proved in vain and the excavation had to be abandoned.

It was nearly half a century before anyone tried again to solve the mystery of what was called the Money Pit. When they did the story was repeated: success so far, then flooding. New shafts were dug to try to drain off the water, but without success.

Not till 1850 did anyone tumble to the truth: the water came from the sea and the daily tides were filling the Pit. A look at the beach nearby revealed a skilfully-constructed drainage system, which allowed the sea to flow downwards into a tunnel running to the Money Pit (a second tunnel was later found too). The putty-sealed platforms had acted as airlocks, holding back the sea until they were broken.

This extraordinary protection for the 'treasure' suggested how valuable it must be and increased men's desire to recover it.

Yet after two hundred years no one has cracked the problem of the Money Pit. New groups claim they'll 'solve it in a jiffy', yet not one jewel or golden coin has been recovered. The ground has been so dug over that the original site has been all but lost. Worse still, a number of treasure-hunters have died in accidents.

Who built the Money Pit, and what was he hiding? Many suggestions have been made, the silliest being that the Pit hides manuscripts which prove that Sir Francis Bacon wrote Shakespeare's plays. The popular view has been the original one, that pirates buried their ill-gotten gains on the island.

One pirate in particular has been mentioned: Captain Kidd. The notorious Kidd was hanged in 1705 for his piracy, but before his execution he had made maps purporting to show his treasure caches. Curiously, one island, marked as in the China Sea, bears a clear resemblance to Oak Island.

But pirates don't have the engineering resources to create something like the Money Pit: it's been estimated that it would have needed 100 men to work for six months to complete it, and some of them would have had to be skilled miners.

Instead it's been suggested by the investigator Rupert Furneaux that an unknown engineering genius created the Pit for the British Army around 1780. The British were then fighting the Americans in the War of Independence and their Commander-in-Chief, Sir Henry Clinton, may have been anxious to build a secure hiding-place for military funds. He could have employed men at his command – known to include a company of Cornish miners – to see to it.

If so, then the likelihood is that the money he stored secretly away was recovered long before Daniel McGinnis made his discovery. Possibly it was never in the Pit at all, but buried near the surface.

In that case, what the unknown engineer created was not a Money Pit but a Money Trap to fool potential robbers, and one which worked beyond expectation: hundreds of thousands of pounds, several lives, and many blighted dreams of wealth have been swallowed up in it.

29

Monsters with Big Feet

When a Sherpa child, living in the Himalayas, misbehaves, its mother will silence it with the warning 'A Yeti is coming'. Is the Yeti – or Abominable Snowman – only a fantasy bogyman, or does it and Bigfoot, the counterpart monster on the west coast of America, really exist?

No bodies or any physical remains have ever been found. But people have claimed to have seen both the Yeti and Bigfoot, and though descriptions inevitably vary a picture can be built up of how the creatures are supposed to look.

Both walk upright and are apelike, with dark or reddish-brown hair except on the face. Bigfoot is the taller at around 2.5 metres, but despite his greater size he is quiet and shy compared with the aggressive Yeti.

Many Yeti incidents are, however, thought to be traceable to bears: bears can stand on their back legs, although they can't walk on two feet.

In fact, since humans can lie or just be mistaken about what they see, almost all the hard evidence for the existence of Yeti and Bigfoot comes from footprints, on the Himalayan mountain snows or along the muddy tracks of the North American pine forests.

One crisp set of Himalayan tracks became for many people the definitive proof of the Yeti's existence. In November 1951, Eric Shipton and Michael Ward, on an Everest expedition, came upon a strange line of footprints. They were exploring a glacier in an unmapped area of Nepal and found that something else had been making its way down before them. They tracked the prints for about a mile and Shipton took a photo of one of the best, with an ice-axe for scale.

This must be the most written-about footprint ever. Clearly some creature made it, but what? It doesn't match any illustrations of animal prints in natural history books. Is it apelike, as some have claimed? Has any distortion been caused by melting in the sunshine?

Whatever tramped across the snow, its print isn't at all like Bigfoot's. His monstrous feet are up to forty-five centimetres long (Shipton's beast had a foot measuring about 33×20 cm) and are much more 'human' in shape. But they are flat-footed compared with human prints and whereas a human walks with toes turning outwards, Bigfoot walks pigeon-toed.

He got his name from Californian journalists in the 1920s, but like the Yeti he has a history going back well before media interest. He is a part of Indian folklore and is known in Canada as the Sasquatch.

Bigfoot or Sasquatch, he has left a lot of prints around. Trails have been discovered of more than 3,000 prints, and while hoaxers with fake feet are known to have stamped their way through the forests, the length and natural appearance of some of these trails are remarkable. One set of prints, discovered by a forest patrolman in 1982, even showed the fingerprint-like lines found on the soles of feet.

If you find it difficult to believe that colonies of monsters can be living largely unobserved in America, you have to remember that the mountainous regions supposed to be their home are remote and vast, with no man-made roads. They are visited only by loggers – and Bigfoot-hunters.

Roger Patterson is one such, and in 1967 he captured what is said to be the best evidence for Bigfoot's reality: six metres of colour film of a lone female. He was riding along Bluff Creek in Northern California when he caught sight of her and, despite being thrown from his terrified horse, managed to roll his camera until the creature disappeared into the forest.

The film has been run and rerun by experts. Most think that if it's a fake then it's a very good one. But there are disquieting features.

Firstly, Patterson says he can't remember the film speed he used: if it was eighteen frames per second then the movements are non-human. But if it was twenty-four frames per second then the she-monster could be a human in a woolly suit. Secondly, the beast's footprints suggest an animal of about 2.5 metres, but analysts say the height of the creature on the film is much less.

A Yeti photo was taken in March 1986 by Anthony Eldridge, an English long-distance runner. Up in the snows he saw strange footprints and at the end of them a 'large, erect shape perhaps two metres tall'. Unfortunately the photo shows little more than a fuzzy blur in the distance.

The case for the existence of either Yeti or Bigfoot seems unproved. Yet a man as eminent as Lord Hunt (leader of the 1953 Everest-conquering expedition) believes that the Snowman exists, that he has seen its prints and heard its yelping call. We can only wait, with open minds, for more evidence.

30

The Unquiet Grave

Early in the last century, beautiful Barbados in the West Indies was the scene of a mystery story as compelling and uncanny as any horror film.

In those days it was common practice to create a vault where all members of the family could be united in death. At Christ Church on the south coast the wealthy Chase family purchased such a tomb. It was made of cemented coral blocks and it measured four by two metres. The entrance was covered by an immense marble slab which needed several men to move.

Head of the family was Thomas Chase, a slave owner, and a man with a reputation for cruelty.

The first person to be interred was a Mrs Thomasina Goddard, on 31 July 1807. Nearly a year later Thomas Chase's infant daughter, Mary Anna Maria, died, and her small coffin was placed in the tomb.

So far nothing untoward had occurred, but on 6 July 1812 the grave was opened again to receive the body of another of Chase's daughters, Dorcas. She had committed suicide because of her father's harshness, or so it was believed.

This time when the marble slab was hauled aside the mourners received a considerable shock: Mary Anna Maria's coffin had moved to the opposite side of the vault, and Mrs Goddard's seemed to have been 'flung' against a wall.

The family strongly suspected that resentful black slaves had been responsible, despite the black population's superstitious fear of disturbing the dead.

Only a month later Thomas Chase himself was dead. There was fearful anticipation of what might be found when the grave was opened, but nothing had been disturbed.

Then in September 1816 a young boy, Samuel Brewster Ames, died. At his funeral witnesses saw with horror that the coffins had again moved. The boy's coffin was quickly put down and the grave closed up. Only two months later it was opened again to receive the remains of another, older Samuel Brewster. He had been buried elsewhere but was now being reinterred.

News of the strange happenings in the tomb had spread far and wide and enormous crowds gathered to see if anything unnatural had occurred. They were not disappointed: the coffins were once again disordered, and Mrs Goddard's had begun to fall apart. Investigators tested walls, floor and roof, but found all solid. Once more the coffins were positioned and this time the marble slab was cemented in place.

Over the next three years thousands of visitors came to get a thrill by looking at the Chase tomb. When the next family member to die, Thomasina Clarke, was to be buried on 17 July 1819 huge crowds came to the funeral, including the Governor of Barbados, Viscount Combermere.

Every coffin, except Mrs Goddard's, had shifted position.

The Viscount now took charge. Mrs Goddard's coffin was left where it was, but the other six were placed in an orderly way: all with their narrow ends pointing to the entrance, and with the three smaller coffins on top of the three larger. Sand was sprinkled on the floor to pick up any footprints. The slab was again cemented in place, and the Viscount marked it with his own seal. No tampering would be possible.

Excitement was at fever pitch, and since no one in the family conveniently died, a decision was taken to examine the tomb again, on 18 April 1820. Crowds gathered as before, and a highly nervous team of local workers prepared to move the slab aside. The seal was unbroken.

Once again the coffins were in jumbled confusion. A decision was at once taken to remove the coffins and reinter them elsewhere, since when all seven have rested in peace.

Is there a natural explanation for what happened? The coffins were all lead-lined, so very heavy. Considerable force would have been needed to move them. Such coffins can move if floated by flood water, but this churchyard was high and dry. Barbados is in an earthquake zone but an earthquake would not produce so localized an effect.

Lead is not influenced by magnetism, but it has been argued that some kind of earth force swung the coffins round. This theory, however, doesn't explain reports that Mary Anna Maria's coffin had hit the wall with enough force to dent it.

The Chase family tomb is still a tourist sight though it's been empty and open now for nearly two hundred years. Leaves blow in and insects fly in and out, but the sinister forces seem to have been stilled.

31

Who Was William Shakespeare?

Perhaps this seems a silly question to ask. After all, everyone knows that William Shakespeare was an English playwright, perhaps the greatest dramatist ever. But for all the fame of his plays the amount of hard fact that we know about Shakespeare could be written on the back of

Alas, poor Shakespeare, we didn't know him too well.

a postcard. Biographies have to be padded out with a lot of guesswork.

Because we know so little about him, people have suggested alternative 'Shakespeares': Christopher Marlowe, for example, a playwright who died in a tavern brawl. Perhaps he didn't die, it's suggested, but lived on secretly, penning plays in the name of an obscure actor called Shakespeare.

An American scholar has analysed portraits of Queen Elizabeth I and Shakespeare recently and decided that they are one and the same person, so *she* wrote the plays!

If we accept that Shakespeare *was* the dramatist, then we come to the mysteries surrounding what's known of his life. A small one to begin with: he was christened in the parish church of Stratford-upon-Avon on 26 April 1564, but on what day was he actually born?

Traditionally we celebrate his birthday on 23 April,

because it's the day of England's patron saint, St George, and also the date of his death in the year 1616 (rather sad, to die on one's birthday, if 23 April is right).

We guess that Shakespeare was educated at Stratford's grammar school, where he would have learnt mainly Latin. He probably didn't enjoy it much, judging from his description in *As You Like It* of 'the whining school-boy with his satchel/And shining morning face, creeping like a snail/Unwillingly to school'.

The next fact is that he got married. He was eighteen years old and married a woman eight years older, called Anne Hathaway. We also know that she had a baby, Susanna, only six months later. Building on these facts it's been suggested that Anne, desperate for a husband, trapped William into marriage by getting pregnant.

It's strange that the day before the marriage licence was granted, one was issued to a William Shakespeare and an Anne Whateley – did the scribe get it wrong, or did Shakespeare try to marry someone else before the Hathaway relatives forced him to marry their Anne? Or were there two William Shakespeares?

After Susanna, twins, Hamnet and Judith, were born in 1585. But from then to the mid–1590s, when we start getting references to him in the London theatre, no one knows where Shakespeare was or what he was doing.

A legend says that he ran away from Stratford because he'd been deer-poaching; other ideas, based on the knowledge he shows in his plays, are that he was a school-master, a lawyer, a soldier, a sailor. It's rather like the game of counting cherry-stones!

How did Shakespeare ever get involved in the theatre? Again, no one knows, though there is a legend that he started out as a kind of parking attendant – looking after the horses of men who had come to see a play.

Apart from plays Shakespeare wrote poems, and here the biggest mysteries lie. At the beginning of his career he published a poem, 'Venus and Adonis', with a dedication to the young, handsome Earl of Southampton, Henry Wriothesley. No one knows how this great lord came to patronize an unknown writer.

Another poem was also dedicated to Southampton. Later a series of sonnets (fourteen-lined poems) were dedicated to 'Mr W. H.'. Who was he? Henry Wriothesley, with his initials reversed? Or someone else?

The sonnets seem to tell a personal story, of himself, a fair young man, and a 'dark lady' who betrays the poet. It's tantalizing to speculate about the identity of these characters and one could almost say that lifetimes have been spent trying to track them down. But we're unlikely ever to know who they were – or even to know if the sonnets describe real experiences or are just fiction, like the plays.

When he retired from the theatre Shakespeare went back to Stratford to the grand house he had bought earlier (for the princely sum of £60!). At his death he left his property to his daughters (Hamnet had died when only eleven years old). Yet neither Susanna nor Judith seems to have been able to write her own name – how could the creator of clever women like Portia and Rosalind have allowed his daughters to remain illiterate?

Shakespeare's will forms the last mystery of his life. In a phrase apparently added as an afterthought he says: 'Item. I give unto my wife my second-best bed with the furniture' (that means the hangings, blankets and so on).

Was this a deliberate insult to Anne? Or a kindly thought because the second-best bed was the comfortable one? Once again we can make guesses, but we're never going to know for certain.

32

The Dingo Baby Case

Ayers Rock in central Australia is one of the most dramatic sights in the world. Beautiful but imposing, it rises 348 metres above the dry plain and is nine kilometres in circumference. For the Aboriginals the rock is sacred. Perhaps it is appropriate that this stupendous rock should have been the setting for Australia's greatest recent mystery.

Tourists flock to Ayers Rock, and among them in

August 1980 were Michael and Lindy Chamberlain, and their children: Aidan, aged six, Reagan, aged four, and a nine-month-old baby girl, Azaria. Michael was a pastor for the Seventh Day Adventist Church, a Christian group who believe that Jesus will one day return in person in this world.

On the evening of 16 August they arrived at the camp-site in their bright yellow hatchback and pitched their tent beside it. Next day the boys and their father climbed the rock while Lindy stayed with her baby, exploring around the base.

That night, after Reagan had gone to bed, the others joined fellow-campers at a barbecue. When Lindy was sure Azaria was asleep in her arms she took her and Aidan back to the tent, but a little later returned with Aidan who was hungry. While she was heating some baked beans one of the other women heard the distressed cry of a baby. Lindy hurried back to the tent.

According to her later testimony, as she got there she saw a dingo (a large doglike animal) leaving the tent. It had something it its mouth which it was shaking. In terror she looked into the tent: blankets were strewn across the floor, and worse – the baby's carry-cot was empty. She ran out and screamed, 'A dingo has got my baby!'

Despite frantic searching Azaria was never seen again. Thus, tragically, began a story which led to the trial and conviction for the murder of her baby of Lindy Chamberlain, and her husband's conviction for having helped her to conceal it. Lindy was sentenced to life imprisonment, though in 1986 she was released and cleared of the murder charge.

What made people suspect that she'd made up the

story of the dingo attack? It was largely a matter of what dingos can or can't do. Many were confident that no wild dingo would go into a human tent. They were also sure that dingos couldn't carry a baby weighing over four kilograms, and that a dingo's jaws couldn't open wide enough to grasp a baby by its head.

Some months after Azaria's disappearance her stretch-towelling suit was found, four kilometres away from the campsite. It was blood-stained around the neck and there were cuts in the fabric. It was argued that a dingo could never have got the body neatly out of the suit (the poppers were undone down the front and right leg, and the bootees were still in the toes).

Although dingos are unknown in Britain, a British scientist's view that an animal could not have made the cuts was much respected. He stated that a knife or scissors had been used.

What exactly was Lindy supposed to have done? Despite the presence of Aidan when she went back to the tent with Azaria, she was believed to have taken the baby into the car, cut her throat, then concealed the body in a bag. She staged the 'dingo has got my baby' scene before telling her husband what really happened. Later they were supposed to have buried Azaria, and dumped the clothing.

Much ugly rumour circulated in Australia about the Chamberlains. Lindy was said to be showing no distress, and there were dark mutterings about the name Azaria: it was said to mean 'Sacrifice in the wilderness' – though it really means 'Blessed by God'.

Forensic scientists claimed that there were substantial traces of blood in the car, blood which could only have come from a baby. Their tests were complicated and controversial, but the trial jury accepted the results and found Lindy guilty.

After she had been sent to prison – where she gave birth to another daughter which was immediately taken away from her – the tide of opinion began to turn in her favour.

Animal experts proved that dingos *can* carry heavy loads, *can* grasp something the size of a baby's head in their jaws, *can* undo a baby's suit without tearing it (a dingo was shown to have unwrapped a chocolate bar without much damage to the silver foil). Dingos *can* cut through cloth in a way which looks like knife slashes.

A family came forward to say that, two months before Azaria's disappearance, they had rescued their two-year-old daughter from a dingo which had dragged her from their car at Ayers Rock. Finally, the 'baby's blood' in the car was shown not to be blood at all. The trial verdict could not stand.

Some people still prefer to believe the dingo innocent rather than Lindy Chamberlain. Perhaps her biggest mistake was in not giving her child an acceptable 'Australian' name. Would there have been the same suspicion if Azaria had been called Charlene or Kylie?

33

The Lost Kingdom of Atlantis

Atlantis: a kingdom under the sea, its pleasant pastures turned to slimy ooze, its houses homes to fishes, its gold-pinnacled temple to the sea-god Poseidon claimed for his watery domain.

This picture of a once prosperous civilization engulfed by water has captured imaginations for hundreds of years, and many people have sought to identify its whereabouts.

The story of Atlantis was told by the Greek philosopher Plato around 350 BC. He learnt it from a manuscript left by his ancestor Solon about 200 years earlier. Solon, in his turn, heard and recorded the tale from an Egyptian priest. And the priest read it in the hieroglyphic records, and told Solon that the events occurred 9,000 years ago!

Plato – reporting Solon reporting the Egyptian priest – says that 'in front of the mouth which you Greeks call, as you say, the pillars of Hercules, there lay an island which was larger than Libya and Asia together'. It was a 'hallowed island . . . of marvellous beauty and endless abundance'.

Yet in the end the kingdom perished, first defeated by the Greeks in battle, then by earthquake and flood when 'on one grievous day and night' the warrior Greeks were 'swallowed up by the earth, and the island of Atlantis in like manner was swallowed up by the sea and vanished'.

Why should we accept any of this as fact rather than fiction? In the first place because Plato insisted that it was. We know from other sources that Solon did visit Egypt, and we know that the Egyptians did keep historical records going back a very long way.

So, if Atlantis existed, where might it be? The reference to the pillars of Hercules, which are at the Straits of Gibraltar, places it out in the Atlantic Ocean. In the last century, when the underwater mid-Atlantic ridge of mountains was discovered, it was suggested that this was the remains of the lost kingdom.

Unfortunately, we now know that it is geologically impossible that the ridge was ever a continent above water.

There have been over forty other suggestions for the location of Atlantis, from Greenland in the cold north, to Australia in the southern hemisphere. Bids have been made for Britain and America, and UFO lovers have been sure that the Atlanteans came from outer space.

The islands of the West Indies have been a popular choice for many, despite the difficulty of believing that an attack against ancient Greece could have been launched from that distance.

More convincingly (though ignoring the placing beyond Gibraltar) Atlantis has been identified with the ancient Minoan civilization found on Crete and other Greek islands. The Minoans were a successful and colourful race who built beautiful palaces and, like the Atlanteans, enjoyed the good things of life. Their civilization did end suddenly.

One Minoan island, Thera (today's Santorini), blew up around 1650 BC in probably the most powerful volcanic explosion in recorded time, causing a huge tidal wave. For a long time it was thought to have overwhelmed Crete, suggesting that Crete was the Egyptian priest's Atlantis.

But, however devastating the eruption, it's been proved that the Minoan palaces in Crete continued to flourish for many years afterwards.

Now a new idea has been proposed by a geo-archaeologist, Eberhard Zangger. He suggests that Atlantis was Troy, and the battle between the ancient Greeks and the Atlanteans, after which Atlantis perished, was the Trojan war. The god Atlas was said to be founder of Troy, so the Egyptians could have known the Trojans as Atlanteans.

The tale of the siege of Troy by the Greeks, though not recorded historically, was told in very ancient times by the Greek poet Homer. In his account the ten-year war was ended by the famous stratagem of the wooden horse, with Greek soldiers hiding inside its body until it was within the walls of the city.

One feature of Plato's Atlantis was a pair of springs, one warm, one cold. Homer too speaks of springs at Troy, one steaming hot and one cold as hail. The Atlanteans' love of horses is likewise echoed by Homer's 'horse-taming' Trojans.

The remains of Troy have been found at Hisarlik in Turkey and not far from the narrow straits leading to the Black Sea. Zangger argues that in Solon's time these could have been known as the Pillars of Hercules, for the names were applied to the Straits of Gibraltar only once Greek sailors had found them.

Archaeologists have shown that ancient Troy was struck by an earthquake, as was Atlantis. But it isn't an island (Zangger suggests the Egyptians weren't good at geography), and it isn't underwater. So the search will probably continue for the coral-encrusted pillars and seaweed-strewn halls of the drowned kingdom of Atlantis.

34

The Parachute Robbery

Over the years there have been many daring criminals, but surely never one more audacious than D. B. Cooper in America. He chose Thanksgiving Day, 24 November 1971, to parachute out of an aircraft with a ransom of

$200,000. Despite an intense search he was never seen again, and no one has ever been able to establish who he really was.

He booked his flight in the name of 'Dan Cooper', though the newspapers got hold of the D. B. Cooper alias, which has stuck. He appeared to be an ordinary middle-aged man in a business suit, wearing dark glasses, when he boarded a Boeing 727 on a flight to Seattle from Portland in Oregon State. There were thirty-six other passengers and a crew of six.

Cooper sat at the back of the plane and all seemed normal until he called one of the stewardesses. He showed her his brief-case, in which she could see wires and two red cylinders. He told her it contained dynamite, and that he would blow up the plane unless his demands were met. He wanted $200,000 and four parachutes, to be put on board at Seattle.

The news was relayed to Seattle and airline workers scurried to try to raise the money and the parachutes. Darkness had fallen by the time the plane landed. Cooper allowed the passengers to leave once the money was on board, but he became increasingly edgy over delays in refuelling. 'He's getting awfully antsy,' reported the captain, William Scott.

When military parachutes were offered he rejected them, insisting on sports models. The difference is that military parachutes open automatically, but with sports models sky divers can free fall as long as they want before pulling the rip-cord.

Cooper tied the bag of money to his belt and made further demands: the steps of the plane were to be lowered once it was in flight, the rear-exit door was to be kept open, and the altitude held at 10,000 feet. He had chosen the plane carefully: the 727 is the only commercial jet from which it is safe to parachute, because the rear exit is behind and under the engines.

After take-off Cooper locked the crew in their cabin. The 727's agreed destination was Reno in Nevada, but when it landed Cooper had gone. The Boeing had been tailed by other aircraft, but the bailing-out had gone unobserved.

Cooper's insistence on sports parachutes with which he could free fall so that his landing couldn't be pin-pointed, was just another indication of how carefully he had planned the operation. It was thought he had demanded four parachutes to give the impression that he would force some of the crew to jump with him, and so stop the authorities giving him a dud parachute.

A great man-hunt followed. The search concentrated on the spot thought most likely for his bail-out, a forest area north of Portland. It was rugged and difficult terrain and nothing was found. The FBI man put in charge of the case was Ralph Himmelsbach, a former fighter-pilot who had been one of those fruitlessly trailing the 727. Over the next eight years he followed up numerous leads, investigating over a thousand men who might have been D. B. Cooper but weren't.

Not a single real clue emerged in all those years until, just seventeen days before Himmelsbach was due to retire, the first and only breakthrough occurred.

On 10 February 1980 the Ingram family were picnicking on a sandy beach on the Colombia River. While his father was building a fire eight-year-old Brian dug in the sand. Suddenly he called his father over: he'd scooped up several bundles of $20 bills. They were in a poor state, but when handed over to the FBI proved to have the serial numbers of notes given to Cooper. The money amounted to over $3,000, and more notes were afterwards found in the same spot.

Had Cooper buried them there, or had the river swept them to the bank, where they'd been covered with sand?

The discovery of the money strengthened the feeling Himmelsbach had had all along that Cooper never survived his jump. It had been a freezing, windy night, and he was wearing only a lightweight suit. However much money he had taken it wouldn't have protected him from the cold.

It is possible that he landed in the river and was drowned, while the money was swept out of the bag in its bundles. But no body has ever been found.

In the town of Ariel, the place nearest to where he is believed to have bailed out, D. B. Cooper now has legendary status. Songs and books have been written about him, there's a museum in his name, and you can buy a D. B. Cooper T-shirt. Every 24 November the townsfolk celebrate the anniversary of the jump. For them Cooper is not a rogue but a hero, and they hope he's enjoying the comfortable life they feel his daring deserved.

35

Nostradamus and his Prophecies

Rochdale United to be promoted! It doesn't seem possible...

When Mr Gorbachev fell from power in Russia it wasn't long before someone claimed that Nostradamus had predicted the event more than four centuries ago.

Could someone who lived four hundred years ago really have seen so far into the future?

Michel de Nostradame was born in 1503 in St Remy de Provence and he died in 1566. His cleverness was recognized at an early age, and he soon mastered Latin, Greek, Hebrew, Mathematics and Astrology.

When he was nineteen he was sent to study medicine, and then for many years he practised as a doctor, journeying over France in his distinctive dark cap and gown. Nostradamus (known by the Latin form of his name) became famous for the help he gave to victims of the plague, a terrible disease which killed thousands – including, tragically, his own wife and children.

He also became known for his uncanny ability to predict the future, as when he knelt in front of an unknown monk and called him 'Your Holiness'. This man later became Pope.

Nostradamus married again, and started to develop his prophetic powers. He had a room at the top of his house converted into a study, and worked at night, gazing intently into a bowl of water placed on a tripod until visions of the future were revealed on its surface.

These he described in verses deliberately made difficult to understand because he feared being burnt at the stake as a magician. But when the first of his verses were published, Nostradamus's fame spread. He was summoned to the court of Queen Catherine de' Medici.

She asked him particularly about a verse which appeared to foretell the death of the King, Henri II, one of whose emblems was a lion. It said:

> Le lion jeune le vieux surmontera,
> En champ bellique par singulier duelle:
> Dans caige d'or les yeux lui crevera,
> Deux classes une, puis mourir, mort cruelle.

(The young lion will overcome the old, in a field of combat in a single fight: he will pierce his eyes in their golden cage; two wounds in one, then to die, a cruel death.)

Nostradamus gave Catherine a tactful answer, but in 1559 the prophecy appeared to be fulfilled. Henri was pierced twice through his golden helmet during a duel with a young Scottish officer (the Scottish crest is a lion), and died in agony.

When a year later Nostradamus's prediction of the early death of Henri's eldest son came true, his reputation was assured. His *Prophecies* have been consulted ever since, despite being very difficult to understand. Very few dates are given to what are mainly forecasts of doom and gloom.

Some verses do seem to point to particular events. The forty-ninth verse of one book reads: 'The Parliament of London will put their king to death.' Charles I was executed by parliamentary order in 1649. 'The blood of the just will be demanded of London, burnt by fire in three times twenty plus six' has been taken as referring to the Great Fire of 1666. Are these predictions just lucky coincidences?

References to the French Revolution and the rise and fall of Napoleon are identifiable, and there are predictions of a German tyrant called 'Hister'.

In another verse Nostradamus tells us that 'Pasteur will be celebrated as a godlike figure. This is when the moon completes her great cycle'. In 1889, the year when Louis Pasteur founded the Pasteur Institute, the moon completed one of its 18.6-year cycles.

But you have to stretch your imagination to connect the next verse, 'The great man will be struck down in the day by a thunderbolt . . . another falls at night-time', with the assassinations of American President J. F. Kennedy and his brother Robert, as has been claimed.

The 'Hister' references gave the Nazis an idea, when they were preparing to invade France in 1940. They circulated made-up verses to indicate that south-eastern France would be safe from war: such was the faith in

Nostradamus that many French civilians fled south, making the north easier to invade. (In a tit for tat move British Intelligence dropped doctored verses over Germany, forecasting German defeat.)

We'll be able to test Nostradamus's powers before long: in one of the few dated verses he says that 'In the year 1999 and seven months, from the sky will come the great King of Terror'. It's a nasty thought: let's hope he got it wrong!

36

Pink Flamingos and Green Sheep

Sometimes the simplest questions create the most knotty problems. We all know why camels have humps, elephants trunks, and leopards spots (or if we don't, we can find out by reading Kipling's *Just So Stories*), but have you ever wondered why flamingos stand on one leg? They certainly look extremely odd, their bright pink bodies balanced on long, spindly legs.

Perhaps Alice could have found out from her croquet mallet flamingo, but it was being rather awkward at the time of her match with the Queen of Hearts, so it was left to the readers of the *New Scientist* magazine to try to solve the problem. In July 1991 it was put to them by Kathy Marthan of Derby, who said it was causing a lot of dispute in her office.

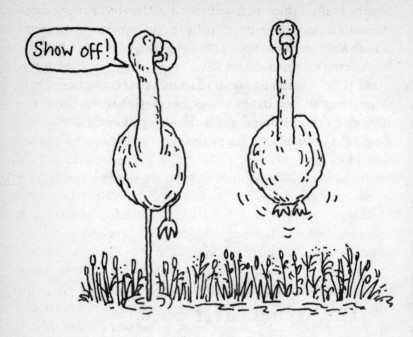

All the way from Japan came one answer – 'So ducks only bump into them half the time'.

Simon Pickering, of the Wildfowl and Wetlands Trust at Slimbridge, wrote more seriously. He said that it is the question most frequently asked by their visitors. At Slimbridge they had had a theory that in winter standing on one leg would halve the heat loss, but observation had showed that the birds' behaviour was the same, summer or winter.

He also pointed out that many other water-birds stand on one leg, even heavy swans, and that humans too tend to change the weight from one leg to another when standing for any length of time. Why do we do that? he asked.

A London reader had noticed that the birds, like humans, don't always stand on the same leg, but alternate them. He felt it would help the birds avoid getting both feet stuck in muddy river bottoms (or humans from sticking to the pavement?).

A letter from an Irish University suggested that it is hard for the veins to pump the blood back up those long, long legs, so standing on only one of them reduces the distance that the blood has to travel against gravity.

An Australian scientist described how Aboriginals hunting kangaroos stand on one leg with their second foot resting on the knee. Apparently kangaroos can't recognize them as hunters in this position! The connection with flamingos wasn't clear, as they are hunted rather than hunters, but it was suggested that one-leggedness 'might confuse the predators'.

Explanations were getting far-fetched, but there were more to come. Maybe the one leg lets the birds sway with the wind; maybe the non-standing leg shows the flamingo to be in a half-sleep stage, resting, as some animals do, with one half of the brain at a time in order to maintain alertness.

At this point readers might have been asked if they'd noticed if flamingos carry anything in the raised foot: in medieval times people believed that resting cranes, similarly long-legged birds, place one of their number on sentry duty. It stands on one leg, clutching a pebble in the other, so that if it dozes off, it'll drop the pebble and wake itself up.

With a final letter suggesting that the birds just got bored with standing on two legs, the Editor of *New Scientist* cried 'Enough!' and called a halt to the correspondence.

But soon a new problem was offered the scientists. A reader asked for help in solving a question which puzzled him and his daughter: why aren't sheep *green*?

It's a reasonable query, when you think about it. Silly sheep in their woolly white coats seem almost to advertise themselves to the wicked wolf.

One reader responded by arguing that animals are at greatest risk when alone. Sheep are most likely to be isolated in snow-drifts, where their white coats disguise them well.

Another writer felt that sheep are already well camouflaged against the grey rocks of the moors and mountains where they live. Each, he claimed, looks like 'a small rocky outcrop against a green background', offering a challenge to unwary walkers who may inadvertently try to stand on one.

In any case, argued Derek Mayell, animals see in black and white (a matador's red cape looks dark grey to a bull), and a whitish-grey sheep looks much the same as a green one to another animal. In his view the question was the wrong one: 'As mammalian predators hunt by scent until they are very close, the question should have been – why don't sheep smell like grass?'

Back to the original problem though. One reader wondered if there *are* green sheep, but no one has ever noticed them.

Tony Howard hadn't forgotten the flamingos. He is sure that being white is a defence mechanism against ducks. With four legs sheep are 'four times more likely than a flamingo to be bumped into by ducks'. And, he went on, 'if green sheep ever evolved, they would suffer substantially greater inconvenience against a background of duckweed, thus provoking even more collisions.' As a final argument that is unanswerable!

The Building of Stonehenge

In the middle of Salisbury Plain stands Britain's most remarkable prehistoric monument: Stonehenge. Though many stones of the great circle have fallen, enough remain to show the grandeur of the builders' original design.

Using only stone hammers, they shaped thirty stones, each six to seven tons in weight, to size before raising them to upright positions in a symmetrical ring. More huge blocks were formed to the right degree of curve to crown the top, each when lifted into position neatly interlocking with its neighbour. A horseshoe of five triliths (a trilith consists of two upright stones and a lintel) was erected within the circle.

Who created this impressive monument? When, how, and for what purpose?

In the medieval period it was believed that King Arthur's magician, Merlin, transported the stones from Ireland and built Stonehenge by magic. Later generations suggested that only the Romans who conquered Celtic Britain in the first century AD would have had the skill to raise the stones.

Then in the eighteenth century a new idea took root: that Stonehenge was a place of worship for the Druids. Druids, priests of the Celts, were a strange group whose rituals involved human sacrifice, so people shuddered to think what might have gone on there. But we now know that Stonehenge is much, much older than the Druids. Radio-carbon dating has proved that the stone circle was built as far back from the Druids' time as we are from theirs.

We also know that it wasn't built all at once. At first, around 2800 BC, a ditch surrounding a circle of ground was all that was created, perhaps with wooden posts or buildings. At a later stage a circle of so-called 'blue-stones' was begun within, but abandoned before it was finished.

Then in about 2000 BC, during what is called the Bronze Age, the great structure we know today was raised, with the blue-stones forming a smaller circle inside the larger one.

These seven-ton blue-stones pose a problem, since they must have come from sites in Wales. How could primitive peoples, without wheeled transport, have moved them over 200 miles across country? It's been suggested that they were 'floated' by sea and river; to prove it could have been done, in 1954 boys from Bryanston and Canford Schools ferried a cement replica stone to Salisbury

Plain, hauling it between waterways on rollers.

But now it's thought that the stones may have been on Salisbury Plain in the first place, deposited by glaciers in the last ice-age. Even so, their collection, and that of the main building blocks – sarsen stones from the Marlborough Downs over twenty miles away – would have been an enormous undertaking.

It's been reckoned that it would have taken 100 to 150 fit young men to drag each sarsen to position. The uprights, when shaped, would have been levered into holes and then hauled vertical. Getting the lintels on top would have been much more difficult, perhaps involving raising them slowly on log and earth platforms.

We have, therefore, a clear idea of when and a fairly good idea of how, but what was Stonehenge for? This is the great debating point today.

The argument centres on just how clever we believe Stonehenge's builders were. It's long been known that the entrance to Stonehenge was aligned with the midsummer sunrise and the midwinter sunset. So, was Stonehenge a place of worship of the sun, marking the passage of the seasons in a fairly simple way, or was there more to it than that?

Outside the main circle there are four small stones called the Station Stones, set up in a rectangle whose short sides also point to the midsummer and midwinter rising and setting suns.

Is it by coincidence or design that the long sides point to the most southerly rising and most northerly setting of the moon? This is a cycle of events which takes eighteen and a half years: at a time before anyone could write and when life expectancy was only twenty-five to thirty years, can we believe that the builders had acquired such

137

sophisticated knowledge?

Considering the skill which went into the engineering of the circle we should beware of underestimating Bronze Age man. But some commentators go further and claim that Stonehenge is in effect an astronomical computer for making complicated calculations about the movements of sun, moon and stars.

However, others reject this theory, pointing out that there are so many stones that just by coincidence they are bound to line up with heavenly bodies.

Stonehenge today is a busy place, visited by a million tourists a year – that is a hundred times the entire population of Britain when Stonehenge was built. Yet the mystery remains. Temple or observatory? We'll probably never know for sure.

38

What Happened to Amelia Earhart?

When in 1937 the American woman pilot Amelia Earhart set off to try to be the first woman to fly round the world, the whole of the world followed her progress. Then her plane disappeared in the Pacific and the world was stunned. What had gone wrong?

Amelia had become the darling of the press in 1928 when she'd been the first woman to cross the Atlantic in an aircraft, although only as a passenger. But in 1932

she did make the first ever solo woman's crossing of the Atlantic.

It wasn't a comfortable flight: she had to suffer the noise and vibration of the engines, and was tossed around in the turbulent air – planes then could not reach the high altitudes which make for smooth flights today. It was twenty hours and forty-nine minutes before, with relief, she spotted land ahead.

More daring pioneering flights followed until in 1936 Amelia said she had only one more goal – a round-the-world flight. Her husband, the publisher George Putnam, encouraged her and helped raise the money to finance the trip.

The main problem and danger of Amelia's plan was the Pacific crossing. After Honolulu in Hawaii 3,900 miles of ocean stretched ahead, beyond her Lockheed Electra's fuel capacity. She had to plan a landing on Howland Island, two and a half miles long and half a mile wide, in mid-Pacific. Finding this speck in the ocean would be very different from looking for the British Isles.

So she decided not to go alone but to take a navigator, Fred Noonan, with her. They left California on St Patrick's Day, 17 March 1937, with Noonan sporting a bunch of shamrock for luck. But luck deserted them at Honolulu where the plane crashed on take-off for Howland. Undeterred, Amelia decided to try again, but this time to go in the other direction.

Keeping close to the equator they flew first to South America then to Africa, India, SE Asia, and Australia. Next stop was Lae in Papua New Guinea, reached on 29 June after a journey of 22,000 miles. By now both were very tired. Planes were still noisy, slow-flying, and uncomfortable – Amelia's cockpit measured just one and a half metres in both directions. Unfortunately, the difficult Pacific leg of their journey was still to come.

On 2 July they left for Howland Island. To help her locate it, the US Navy had stationed a coastguard vessel, the *Itasca*, close by, and Amelia was to broadcast messages as soon as her two-way radio was near enough to make contact. With relief the radio operators first faintly picked up her voice eighteen hours and forty-five minutes after take-off.

As she drew closer her voice was heard more clearly, but there was a problem. They could hear her but only once did Amelia seem to be able to hear them, and they couldn't get a radio fix to establish her position. Tension in the radio room mounted when she told them that her fuel was running low.

She was circling at 1,000 feet but said she couldn't see the island or the ship – which was sending up thick black smoke to make itself visible. A last, clearly anxious, call came through twenty hours and fourteen minutes after her take-off, then silence.

A massive search operation began, in the hope that Amelia had been able to launch the life-raft after ditching. For three days afterwards radio signals were picked up which were thought to come from the Lockheed. But nothing was found and it was sadly concluded that she and Fred had died with the impact on the water, and that the plane had now sunk.

There the story rested till the 1940s when America and Japan were fighting in the Pacific during the Second World War. Then rumours started to circulate that Amelia wasn't dead, but a prisoner on the Japanese-held Marshall Islands. It was claimed she had been captured when she ditched, because she'd made a detour over forbidden territory to spy for the US government.

The end of the war didn't stop the rumours. In fact they increased when Marshall islanders told of a Caucasian woman with a male companion who'd been on the islands. One witness swore that she'd heard the shots of their execution. Others said that the woman had died of dysentery.

The American government gave assurances that Amelia had not been spying, though not everyone believed them. But it isn't very likely: she was well aware of the riskiness of her journey without complicating it further.

In 1991 new light was thrown on this old mystery when a piece of what is claimed to be Amelia's plane was discovered on the desert island of Nikumaroro, south of Howland Island. An American size nine shoe, said to be hers, has also been found. Richard Gillespie, the investigator, hopes to return to look for remains of bodies, believing that Amelia and Fred probably survived a crash-landing on the island but then died of thirst.

But why wasn't the wreckage spotted by search teams that overflew the island? Could Amelia have been taken prisoner by the Japanese after all? The new evidence hasn't answered all the questions set when Amelia's brave adventure turned to tragedy.

39

Animals that Shouldn't be Here

How would you feel if, like twelve-year-old Kay Hall of Caerphilly in March 1978, you went round the back of your house and found a one and a half metre crocodile lying there – even if it was dead? Or if driving along the M55 in Lancashire you spotted a living crocodile dashing across the carriageway in front of your car, as happened to startled motorists in May 1980?

But it isn't just crocodiles that suddenly appear in our gardens, on our roads, or in our woods and fields. All kinds of creatures that we normally only expect to see on our TV screens have been turning up without explanation.

In 1984, for example, a giant fruit bat with a wing-span a metre across was discovered clinging to a car radiator in the middle of Exeter in Devon. How an animal normally found in New Guinea got to Britain remains a mystery.

Wild boars are supposed to have been extinct in Britain for 400 years, yet in the 1970s one or more boars were making a nuisance of themselves in the Odiham area of Hampshire, digging up people's gardens and eating young trees. Another, seen but never caught, did a lot of damage to gardens in Basildon, Essex, in 1979.

Land animals aren't the only oddities. In September 1983 Alan Clarke and his father were swimming in the River Leven in Cumbria when a huge fish with a swordfish spike leapt out of the water. They watched it leaping until it dashed itself on to rocks. It was later identified as a marlin, a fish not of fresh water but normally found in the seas off Africa.

Other creatures which shouldn't have been here but were include wolves, bears, lions, jackals, monkeys, hyenas, emus, a variety of snakes, and even an Arctic fox.

The usual explanations for these strange sightings are that the animals have escaped from zoos, circuses or private owners. Some must be former 'pets', perhaps abandoned by owners who no longer want them, but zoos and circuses do want their animals back and make no secret of it if one gets away.

A wilder suggestion is what's called 'teleportation': the

idea that the animals are supernaturally transported from jungle, savannah, or wherever it is that they were happily getting on with their lives, to British back gardens, roads or rivers.

Misidentification is a more rational possibility and is the most frequent explanation offered for the many wild cat sightings in Britain since the 1960s. These ABCs (Alien Big Cats) are elusive creatures, frequently seen but rarely caught. Two in particular achieved star status: the Surrey puma, and the Beast of Exmoor.

In the two years following September 1962 police at Godalming in Surrey recorded 362 sightings of a mystery beast, sandy-coloured, with a fierce catlike face, long legs and tail, standing about a metre high. Deer, rabbits and on one occasion a heifer, appear to have been its prey. Police borrowed a cage from London Zoo hoping to catch it, but without luck. Sightings of the puma – if it was a puma – continued for years.

The Beast of Exmoor was a ferocious creature, creating havoc amongst sheep-farms from February 1983 onwards. It eluded numerous attempts to hunt it down, including one by twelve armed marines. There were doubts that it was one of the big cat family though – some considered that it was a vicious dog.

Other big cats have actually been caught. Farmer John Noble of Cannick in Scotland, who had lost a number of sheep to an attacking animal between 1979 and 1980, baited a trap with a sheep's head. Some days later he heard a growling as he went to check the cage and found that he had bagged a female puma! She was sent to a zoo, named Felicity, and became quite an attraction. But where she originated remained a mystery.

More recently, in July 1988, a large cat was run over

on Hayling Island near Portsmouth. The body was picked up by a witness and later identified by Marwell Zoo as that of a North African swamp-cat. How such a creature even got to Britain let alone over the causeway to Hayling Island nobody could discover. Moreover since other sightings followed there may be a whole colony of swamp-cats living on the island!

Some alien animals are known to have established breeding colonies in Britain following escape from captivity. There are wallabies in the Peak District and Ashdown Forest, while racoons live in Kent, and porcupines in woods in Devon. A flock of green parakeets swoops squawking over the Thames in Berkshire as if it was the Amazon.

Explained and unexplained there seem to be many exotic creatures living with us. Maybe we'll next get reports of rhinos running around the Cotswolds, or elephants on the loose in Lanarkshire!

40

Human Lift-off

All of us have had dreams that we can fly. When we wake up we wish that it were true, but we know that the laws of gravity won't allow it. Or will they? Over the centuries hundreds of people have claimed to have witnessed someone levitating, that is, rising apparently weightless from the ground.

In 1657, for example, twelve-year-old Henry Jones of Shepton Mallet is reported to have been seen several times floating up to the ceiling. Once he sailed right over the garden wall.

Devotedly religious people seem more likely to levitate than the rest of us. Joseph of Copertino was made a saint after his death in 1663 because his 'flying', witnessed by many, was seen as a divine gift. Joseph's levitation could be troublesome though: once he flew on to an altar and was badly burned by the candles.

With these stories of long ago, when people believed in magic, we may think that witnesses mistook what they saw. But in our own century there are plenty of stories of levitation.

A famous series of photographs appeared in the *Illustrated London News* in 1936 showing an Indian yogi apparently lying in air. One hand rested on a cloth-covered stick, otherwise, according to the English photographer who looked all round and underneath him, there was absolutely no kind of support.

The freedom the photographer had to walk around and examine makes the case different from the many stage illusions where a lightly-clad girl appears to be floating. Even so, it is because it is possible to create the appearance of levitation by trickery (do you know how? – I don't) that reports of the supposed real thing have to be treated with caution.

The most sensational of all levitators in Britain was Daniel Dunglas Home, and arguments have raged about whether his apparently extraordinary achievements were true or false.

Home, born in Edinburgh in 1833, was a well-known medium – that is, someone supposed to be able to contact a spirit world. He began having psychic experiences when a boy, while living in America. When he was thirteen he believed he'd seen the spirit of a friend, standing at the foot of his bed. Two days later the family indeed received news of the boy's death.

When he got older Home started to hold seances, and it was at one of these, when he was nineteen, that he first levitated. An account was written by a newspaper editor, not the sort of person you'd expect to be easily fooled. The room was dark, but the editor was convinced that Home had risen from the floor without trickery. 'I had hold of his hand at the time,' he wrote, 'and I and others felt his feet – they were lifted a foot from the floor.' Home came down and then went up again – right up till his head bumped the ceiling!

He came to London when he was twenty-two, and was a sensation. People flocked to his seances, most to be impressed, though the poet Robert Browning was sure he was a fraud and wrote a long contemptuous poem, 'Mr Sludge the Medium', about him.

But at the many seances, when strange noises were heard, ghostly hands wove garlands of flowers, heavy tables rose unaided from the floor, and musical instruments played apparently on their own, Home was never caught cheating.

The most talked-about of all Home's levitations occurred on 13 December 1868, when he is supposed to have floated out of an upstairs window and in, feet first, at another. Three men witnessed this, all of them men of repute: Lord Adare, the Master of Lindsay, and Adare's cousin, Captain Charles Wynne.

Doubters have since examined the accounts minutely, to look for evidence that events must really have been different. There are discrepancies between the different versions, though most are not of great importance. But the Master of Lindsay made a grave mistake when he claimed that the moon was bright that night and throwing shadows on the walls. In fact, there was no moon.

One researcher, Archie Jarman, in 1980 identified the house where the 'levitation' had occurred and himself tried to edge across between the two windows, some 13.5 metres above the street. He had to give up the dangerous attempt but he concluded that Home might have managed it if helped by a rope.

But there were many at the time who believed in Home. Sir William Crookes, an eminent scientist, conducted a number of experiments with him and ended by saying that 'there is an antagonism in my mind between *reason*, which pronounces it to be scientifically impossible, and the consciousness that my senses, both of touch and sight, are not lying witnesses'.

Maybe gravity is a law that can be defied. After all, plenty of schoolchildren have successfully tried the trick of getting in a group and with only one finger each and a bit of mumbo-jumbo lifting up a friend. Perhaps you're one of them – if so, you'll probably believe in levitation!

41

The Body in the Bog

On 1 August 1984 a worker at Lindow Moss, an ancient bog near Wilmslow in Cheshire where peat is cut, had a nasty shock. He threw out what he thought was a piece of wood amongst the peat – but as the object hit the ground it was revealed as a human foot!

The police were called, but because it didn't look like a recent bit of body an archaeologist was summoned as well. He realized at once that the foot was indeed very old and he looked for more of the body. It proved quite easy: peat is cut by big machines, and in the side of the section left behind the archaeologist could see a flap of skin sticking out.

In fact, only the upper half of the body remained. The legs had been sliced away (presumably ending up on someone's flower bed!). But the upper half had been well

preserved in the cool moist peat. Pete Marsh, as he was nicknamed, was carefully excavated and carried away for scientific examination.

Who was he? When had he lived? What did he look like, how had he died and why was his body in the bog?

Some of these questions proved easier to answer than others. In the first place, radio-carbon testing established a date of about 300 BC for Lindow Man – his more dignified scientific name. Examination of the teeth suggested an age between twenty-five and thirty years. Despite missing his legs, it was possible to say that he was well-built, probably about 1.7 metres tall. A lifelike reconstruction of his face was made, showing a good-looking man with trimmed beard and moustache.

These details were interesting, but what proved really startling about Lindow Man was the manner of his death.

He had been murdered! Not only had his skull been shattered by blows from a blunt instrument, he had also been garotted by a thin cord. As if that wasn't enough his throat had been cut too.

He was naked except for a fur arm-band. Had he been the victim of some vicious Iron Age muggers who stripped him of all he had before dumping his body in the bog?

The finger-nails were smooth and unchipped, suggesting that he had not had to do hard manual work. Perhaps he was a man of wealth and rank with possessions worth stealing.

Most of the internal organs had not survived the long centuries in the bog, but it proved possible to examine the gut to see what Lindow Man had eaten for his last meal. It appeared to have been a snack rather than a meal, a bread-cake made of wholemeal flour from various cereals. It probably didn't taste very nice for there were little burnt pieces in it.

Lindow Man would be harder to explain if it weren't that other well-preserved 'bog bodies' have been found in northern Europe. Some of these were the result of accidental deaths, some bodies are of much later dates, but two found in Denmark seem to have much in common with our own.

Tolland Man was found in 1950, Grauballe Man in 1952. While Lindow Man's head is squashed in shape, Tolland Man – who died about 2,000 years ago – has a perfectly preserved head. He looks peacefully asleep. But around his neck is a woven noose which had been used to kill him. Like Lindow Man he is naked, apart from a cap on his head and a leather belt.

Grauballe Man, perhaps 200 years younger, looks anything but serene. His facial expression suggests the terror he must have felt when he faced death. His throat was slashed from ear to ear; possibly he had also received a blow to the skull. He too was naked when his body was buried in the bog.

Like Pete Marsh both men had had a last meal, probably of a kind of porridge of different varieties of grain and seed: as many as sixty-three kinds in the case of Grauballe Man.

Here may be the clue to all three men's deaths. Archaeologists believe that the men were sacrificial victims in societies which worshipped the Earth Goddess. It is seen as significant that the 'last meals' were entirely vegetarian, made from the cereal grains planted annually on which the whole community's living depended.

Many objects have been found in Danish bogs, left as gifts to the Earth Mother. She showed her ready acceptance when she swallowed them up. The 'gift' of one of their own kind was her people's grandest gesture – or could it have been a desperate one following a poor harvest?

How were the victims selected? That we'll never know. It may have been by lot, it may have been by seizing someone of another tribe, or it may have been that the choice fell on some high-born man of their own community. The state of the hands and finger-nails of all three perhaps supports this idea.

Willingly or unwillingly, men at Lindow, Tolland and Grauballe probably went to their deaths to ensure the harvest and therefore survival of their peoples. Yet, ironically, it is they who have survived, they whom Mother Earth has preserved through many centuries.

42

Strange Rains

'It's raining cats and dogs,' we say when it pours down. Well, cats and dogs haven't come down yet, but lots of other creatures have: little frogs and toads, snails, snakes, fish, mussels, jellyfish, starfish, worms!

If reports are to be believed, other strange things have fallen too – nuts, peas, beans, seeds, sugar crystals. And there are plenty of reports of uncomfortable showers of stones, clods of earth, and blocks of ice. Pennies and halfpennies are said to have fallen on astonished school-children in Bristol in 1956.

The commonest 'creature' falls, however, are of frogs, toads and small fishes, and they occur all round the world.

On 12 June 1954 Sylvia Mowday was caught in a storm in Sutton Park, Birmingham. Her four-year-old daughter had her little red umbrella up when she heard thudding sounds on it. Her mother described their amazement when they realized they were caught in a shower of frogs: 'The umbrella was covered, our shoulders were covered, and as we looked up we could see the frogs coming down like snowflakes.' They were tiny, but so many fell that they covered an area of about fifty square yards.

In June 1979 Vida McWilliam of Bedford found little frogs all over her garden. She hadn't seen them fall from the sky, so it is possible that they were there beforehand to be brought out by the rain. This explanation is often given for appearances of large numbers of frogs and toads, but in this instance can hardly explain the frog spawn which draped the bushes.

Another explanation for these falls, and those of other watery creatures, is that they have been swept up by whirlwinds or waterspouts, swirled into the upper atmosphere, and later deposited in rain, perhaps many miles from where they were picked up. *Pink* frogs fell on Gloucestershire in 1987, possibly brought in on strong winds from the Sahara.

Whirlwinds are certainly very powerful. My brother's family once watched a dust devil in America sweep up all the plates from a neighbouring picnic table and whirl them higher and higher till they disappeared from sight. Perhaps someone later complained of a shower of picnic plates!

But if the frog rains result from a whirlwind sucking up the contents of a pond, why is it so rare for more than one kind of creature to come down at a time? What has happened to all the other animal- and plant-life of the pond? And how have the tiny creatures survived the ordeal?

Rational explanations get harder as the falls get odder. Mr and Mrs Osborne were walking home from church in Bristol on 13 March 1977 when Mr Osborne heard what he thought was a button popping on to the ground. In fact it was a hazel-nut, and it was followed by a fall of hundreds more from a clear blue sky. 'They were peppering down on the road and bouncing off the cars,' he said. The Osbornes took some home and found them good to eat.

Even more peculiar were the showers of mustard and cress seeds which fell on gardens in Southampton in February 1979. They were followed a few days later by falls of peas and beans.

When we get events as strange as these, some commentators resort to extraterrestrial explanations. It has been suggested that alien spacecraft are gathering up samples of our plants and animals for investigation and dumping what they don't need or have finished with. Alternatively it's been claimed that the aliens are benevolently dropping free gifts!

But if aliens *are* responsible, then not all are well-intentioned. Falling ice and stones have caused much damage. In January 1951 a carpenter on the roof of his house in Düsseldorf in Germany was actually killed by a shaft of ice.

Ice can, of course, form on the wings of planes and then break off, and no doubt this does explain some ice falls. But it could not be the cause of the huge block, six metres in circumference, which fell on the Isle of Skye in 1849.

Another substance which falls but which has never been explained is known as 'angel hair' for its gossamer-like texture. A careful account was written by the Hampshire naturalist Gilbert White in 1741. One September day he noted a 'shower of cobwebs falling from very elevated regions, and continuing without any interruption till the close of day'.

Though it has been suggested that angel hair is the gossamer produced by the spiders which float on currents of air in autumn, White observed that the threads were quite broad (about five centimetres) and that they fell forcefully, not drifting as spiders' webs do.

Unless you choose to believe that aliens are circling the earth and pelting us with nuts or stones for fun, it seems that weather involves much more than sun, wind, and rain. Perhaps one day forecasters will be able to add symbols for frog or jellyfish showers to their weather-maps!

43

Who Was Kaspar Hauser?

Who was Kaspar Hauser, and who had given him such a bad haircut?

← ???

For five years in the nineteenth century Kaspar Hauser was the sensation of Europe. Who was he, where had he come from, for what dark secret had someone tried to kill him? Then in 1833 he *was* killed. Whatever the truth of his identity, it went to the grave with him.

The mystery began late in the afternoon of 26 May 1828. Into the market square of Nuremberg (now part of Germany) hobbled a bedraggled-looking youth, who almost collapsed into the arms of a cobbler. He seemed unable to speak but clutched a letter addressed to the Captain of the Sixth Cavalry regiment.

At the guardhouse he behaved peculiarly, burning himself when he tried to pick up a candle by the flame. He was frightened by a grandfather clock and when beer and meat were offered he recoiled, though he fell ravenously on bread and water.

The envelope contained two letters. One claimed to be written by 'a poor labourer' who gave the boy's name and said he'd been left with him in 1812 by his mother. The other, apparently from the mother, said that she was too poor to look after the baby; his dead father had been a cavalry soldier and she begged that he be taken when he was seventeen to join his father's regiment.

But these letters were not to be trusted: they'd obviously been written at the same time and by the same person.

Kaspar was taken to the local police station and put in a cell. There he seemed quite happy. He would sit still for hours and he prefered darkness to light. He had very few words: when curious people came to gawp at him he was unable to tell men from women – he called everyone 'boy'. All animals were 'horse': someone gave him a toy horse and he loved it, pretending to give it food as if he were a small child.

But he was not mentally retarded: very quickly he began to pick up language, and soon learned to read and write. It wasn't long before he could tell his own story.

Kaspar said that he had been imprisoned all his life in a tiny dark dungeon where he could not stand upright (his legs were, in fact, malformed). Bread and water were left for him while he was asleep. Sometimes his hair would be cut and his bedding changed while he slept.

He saw no one, until the day when a man came in and began to teach him a few words and his name. The same man had dressed him in tattered clothes and led him almost to the gates of Nuremberg. Police searched the countryside seeking information about the man or the house where Kaspar had been held, but without success.

All over Germany people began to talk about Kaspar. He was released from prison into the care of a Professor Daumer, who began to educate him. Then on 7 October 1829 the story took a sensational twist. Kaspar was found unconscious on the floor of Daumer's cellar. He had a wound on his forehead and claimed that a man wearing gloves and a mask had attacked him.

For many people this confirmed that Kaspar was really someone important. Could he be the rightful heir to some grand estate? But when police could find no clues to his attacker others said that Kaspar had wounded himself, wanting even more attention than he'd got already.

In 1831 an English nobleman, Lord Stanhope, took Kaspar under his wing. He toured him round the courts of Europe, parading him in front of royalty. The boy seemed to enjoy the fuss. After two years, however, Stanhope got tired of it and lodged Kaspar in the small town of Ansbach with a new strict tutor, Dr Meyer. Kaspar was very unhappy: he didn't like exchanging the fun of court banquets for Latin lessons.

Then on a cold December day in 1833 Kaspar staggered into Dr Meyer's house with a severe stab wound. He had, he said, been lured to the park by a tall, black-cloaked man. The stranger had given him a wallet, then stabbed him.

The police found the wallet in the park: inside was a very odd and contradictory note written in mirror writing. It said, 'Hauser will be able to tell you how I look, whence I came and who I am . . . I will tell you myself . . . My name is M. L. 0.'

None of it made sense, and suspicion that Kaspar had staged the whole incident grew when police said that the snow in the park had shown only one set of footprints.

But if the wound was self-inflicted Kaspar had misjudged matters for he died two days later. His last words were, 'I didn't do it myself.'

Was Kaspar a fraud or not? Some people think that even the first part of the story doesn't ring true: surely a boy kept in a room in which he couldn't stand upright wouldn't be able to walk at all? Some accept the beginning of the tale but think he was perhaps a 'love-child', the illegitimate son of some poor woman who was afraid to acknowledge him.

Others, however, argue that Kaspar was murdered to prevent discovery of who he really was. It seems right that the inscription on his tombstone reads: 'Kaspar Hauser, Enigma'.

44

The Piltdown Forgery

In 1911 a Sussex solicitor and fossil-hunter, Charles Dawson, dug up part of a skull from a gravel pit near Piltdown Common. Thus began the story of one of the most ingenious crimes this century. We need a Sherlock Holmes to solve it and, strangely enough, his creator Conan Doyle is one of the many suspects. It isn't a murder mystery though, but a tale of archaeological fraud.

Over a century ago Charles Darwin argued that man had not been created but had evolved over millions of years from ape ancestors. From then on archaeologists hunted for fossil remains of the 'missing links', skeletal forms which would show the halfway stages from ape to man.

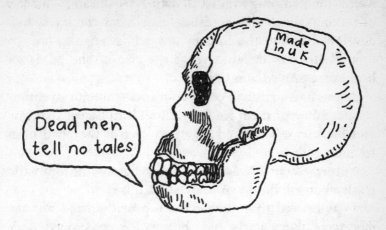

Dawson contacted Sir Arthur Smith Woodward of the British Museum and together with another keen fossil-hunter, a French priest Pierre Teilhard de Chardin, they sifted through the gravel. More bits of skull were unearthed, and the fossil teeth of ancient animals such as hippo, elephant and mastodon.

Then in 1912 there was a vital find. Smith Woodward later told how Dawson was using a tool to dig gently in the bottom of the pit 'when we both saw the half of a human lower jaw fly out'.

It was the right half of an apelike jaw with two teeth remaining – but the teeth looked more human than ape. Greatly excited the men declared that with jaw and top of skull together they'd found the missing link.

Because of the age of the animal fossils Piltdown Man, as he became known, was thought to be about two million years old. Archaeologists in Britain hailed the discovery, proud that these remains were those of the earliest human and that he'd proved to be English!

Perhaps the most eminent of these men was Sir Arthur

Keith. He had long argued that the large brain, which is one thing which distinguishes man from the apes, had developed before the human jaw which enables him to talk. Keith was delighted that the size of the Piltdown brain-case proved him right.

But archaeologists in other countries were not so enthusiastic. Some of them found it difficult to accept that jaw and brain-case belonged together, even if they had been found together.

Nevertheless, it was forty years before the dramatic truth emerged: Piltdown Man was a hoax!

Tests proved that neither the top of the head nor the jaw were particularly old, but had been stained dark brown to look as if they were. While the top of the skull was human, the bit of jaw belonged to an orang-utan, with its teeth filed down to man-size. The genuine fossils found with them came from elsewhere in the world and had been planted too.

Who was the villain of the piece? Dawson (by then dead) was the first suspect, especially when it was discovered that he'd cheated with claimed finds before. But even if guilty it is likely that he was only an accomplice. He couldn't have obtained the real fossils found, and he wouldn't have known how to doctor the jaw so that the vital parts which would have shown that it didn't go with the top of the head were missing.

So what about Sir Arthur Smith Woodward? Did he produce the fakes in order to get some glory? Possible, but unlikely, since he was still looking for fossils at Piltdown in the 1930s. He'd hardly have done so if he'd known there was nothing to find.

Teilhard de Chardin has been a favourite suspect, despite being a priest. He had the opportunity, he had the know-how, and some of the animal teeth came from sites abroad where he had been. Perhaps he wanted to make fools of the British.

Almost every other archaeologist has been looked at for motive and opportunity. Some have been thought to have wanted to expose Smith Woodward to ridicule. But if this was so, you'd have expected them to see that the hoax was found out sooner.

Many amateur archaeologists in Sussex have been suspected, including Sir Arthur Conan Doyle. In his novel *The Lost World* he wrote: 'If you are clever, and you know your business, you can fake a bone as easily as you can fake a photograph.' But there's no real evidence to link him with the Piltdown fake.

Most recently the finger of suspicion has pointed at the most eminent man of them all: Sir Arthur Keith. It's been discovered that he knew Dawson rather better than he claimed, and that he wrote an anonymous article about Piltdown, showing knowledge of the discovery, days before he officially found out about it. Perhaps he couldn't resist the temptation to 'prove' his theories of early man.

So there's a wide choice of suspects – step forward, Sherlock Holmes!

45

Water Witching

Of all the talents humans can be born with, none is more mysterious than dowsing or water-divining, the ability to discover underground water using nothing more than a forked stick or a swinging pendulum. Metals can be located too. No one can explain it, but neither can anyone deny that it works.

Dowsing has a long history and in past times was regarded as a magic art – in America it is still called 'water witching'. Much superstition was attached to selecting and cutting the traditional Y-shaped rod used. Hazel, rowan or ash wood were preferred and it was believed that the sticks should be cut while the moon was new and with the dowser facing east.

But nowadays dowsers make use of almost any material: metal coat-hangers have been shaped, plastic and whalebone have been used, and even, it is said, German sausage!

My father, an amateur dowser, used the conventional rod. He once helped a friend find water for her simple holiday home in Cornish woodland. She had no piped water, and it wasn't much fun lugging cans of drinking-water up a long lane.

My father looked for a nearer supply, and found a spot where he got a vigorous reaction. About a metre below the surface of the ground a spring was found. A basin was dug, natural-looking steps made down to it, and when ferns and other plants had grown it looked as if the little well had been there for centuries.

Incredibly, a true professional dowser can tell not only that there is water beneath his feet, but exactly how far down it is, the quantity, and the rate at which it's flowing. It's no good digging a well which will quickly run dry!

Recent dry winters have left reservoirs empty and given dowsers plenty of work – in 1992, for example, the well-known Cornish dowser, Don Wilkins, helped the people of Bryher in the Scillies to find a supply. He was able to pin-point two sources of water, thirty metres deep in the rock.

One dowser claimed actually to be able to see the

water 'shimmering like green moonlight' through the soil. South African Pieter van Jaarsveld was twelve years old when in 1963 his abilities attracted world-wide attention. He was nicknamed 'the boy with X-ray eyes', but he himself was surprised that no one else could see something he took for granted. He was said also to be able to discover diamonds – a very useful talent!

Dowsers usually find it difficult to explain how they know such things – it seems to be instinctive, perhaps like the instincts which enable birds, fish, butterflies and other creatures to navigate their way over thousands of miles.

Many animals also have the ability to detect underground supplies of water, and it's been suggested that animals with horns or tusks may be using them as dowsing instruments. Elephants are particularly good and generous water-finders, providing for other animals as well as for their own kind. Nature has endowed them with two potential dowsing implements – tusks, and a trunk to use as a pendulum.

The pendulums used by humans are simply made of thread with a weight attached. Dangled over a sensitive object they will swing or gyrate to pass back information to the dowser.

The Japanese apparently use pendulums to determine the sex of chicks still in the egg. Amazingly the pendulum, a simple bead on a silk thread, circles clockwise for a cock chick and anti-clockwise for a hen. It sounds extraordinary, but a ninety-nine per cent success rate is claimed.

Reportedly many other things have been dowsed by pendulum, from buried treasure to dead bodies and even their murderers! But this sort of dowsing is much more controversial than the straightforward water-divining.

Map-divining too is difficult to accept. It is possible to believe, as has been suggested, that some form of magnetism communicates through the ground to a dowser, but this can't apply to dangling a pendulum over a map and asking it to provide information. Yet dowsers claim that it works.

We're told that far more people have the ability to dowse than actually do, but because they've never tried it they don't know that they can. So why not have a go?

For the traditional method you need a pliable Y-shaped twig, with the two arms about thirty centimetres long. With palms upwards and at waist level grasp the arms firmly, pulling them outwards. Then hold the stick parallel to the ground and see if anything happens!

For testing purposes it's as well to know that there is water around, so try on a bridge or where you know there's a drain or water-pipe beneath you. If you're a dowser the stick will pull down, twist and even circle. You could become a living mystery to your friends!

46

Monsters of the Deep

On 6 August 1848 the British naval frigate *Daedalus*, returning home from India, was in the South Atlantic. At five o'clock in the afternoon a young midshipman noticed something strange, and drew attention to it. It was a sea serpent!

Eventually the ship came close enough for the creature

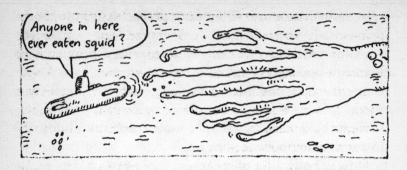

to be made out in detail. It was about eighteen metres long, dark brown, with yellowish throat markings. The head was snakelike, on a neck which jutted a metre above the water. Down its back was a seaweed-like mane.

Captain Peter M'Quhae later described what they'd seen in a letter to *The Times* and caused a sensation – though one old sea-dog declared that the crew of the *Daedalus* had been fooled by a long strand of the seaweed called kelp.

There's been no shortage of claimed sea monsters before or since; some recently sighted have become so familiar that they've been named: there's Morgawr in Cornwall, for example, and Chessie, of Chesapeake Bay in North America.

Morgawr ('Sea Giant') was first spotted in 1975. Two observers watched a creature with hump back and stubby horns come to the surface with a wriggling conger eel. A year later fishermen said they'd seen what they first thought an upturned boat, but which proved to be a dark, humpy back. A big-eyed head rose up before the whole creature sank down again.

Other sightings have followed, though there hasn't been as much agreement about shape and colour as there has across the Atlantic about Chessie.

Chessie – or maybe the Chessies, as some people have

seen more than one – appears to be a dark, smooth-skinned sea serpent, up to ten metres long, swimming with up and down motions that give the impression of humps. Chessie has been compared with the South American anaconda, and it has been suggested that somehow a small colony of anacondas has established itself there, though the anaconda is a freshwater snake and normally likes its swimming water warm.

Undoubtedly a lot of reports of strange sea beasts result from the eye misinterpreting what it sees. In 1857 young Henry Lee on Brighton beach heard two boys shouting 'A sea snake, a sea snake!' He looked up and saw 'a veritable sea monster', with seven fins on its long body. But when older and wiser, he realized that what he'd seen had been seven dolphins, swimming along in a disciplined line.

Even so, no marine scientist would claim that there is nothing yet to be discovered in the oceans. Almost three-quarters of the globe is covered in water, much of it very deep and unexplored. As one scientist put it: 'There are more footsteps on the moon than there are on the sea-bed.'

As recently as 1977 the American Dr Robert Ballard, using his deep-sea submersible, discovered an extraordinary community of creatures.

In the Galapagos rift of the South Pacific, 2,700 metres down, volcanic vents in the ocean floor spew out hydrogen sulphide. This feeds bacteria, which in turn form the food supply of giant clams, mussels thirty centimetres across, and 1.5 metre tube-worms. These are the only creatures in the world which are in no way dependent on the energy of the sun.

Other gigantic sea beasts are known, if rarely seen, like

the great megamouth sharks which cruise the oceans with open mouths the size of doorways. Some species of whale have never been seen alive, although their carcasses have been washed ashore.

But the creatures of the deep which most frighten and fascinate are the giant cephalopods: octopuses and squid. Fearsome tales were told in the past of octopuses overwhelming ships, though the largest octopus actually caught (in 1973) measured 'only' seven metres from the tip of one of its eight arms to another.

The largest-ever squid was a different matter. It was found stranded in 1878 at a place called Thimble Tickle, in Newfoundland. Its eye alone was half a metre across. In addition to eight shortish arms squid have two long tentacles: on a six-metre body this one had tentacles nearly 11 metres long! Suckers on the tentacles were the size of saucers.

Even larger monsters have been seen alive at sea. Silent but deadly battles between giant squid and predatory sperm whales have been watched, the squid's writhing tentacles encircling the whale's great body as it tries to devour its prey.

A fearsome squid was seen by a trawlerman, A. G. Starkey, during the Second World War. On deck one night, in the Indian Ocean, he became aware of a circle of green light below and realized that he was being watched by the 'cold, unblinking' eye of a squid so vast that it stretched the length of the ship. Luckily it merely lay there before sinking out of sight again.

With such creatures known to be in the seas, who would insist that what the crew of the *Daedalus* saw was only a bit of seaweed?

47

The Poor Priest's Treasure

In 1885 a penniless young priest, Berenger Saunière, arrived at an equally poverty-stricken village, Rennes-le-Château, perched on a hilltop in southern France. For several years he struggled to live on a tiny income, and to keep the crumbling thousand-year-old church from falling into ruin.

Then, suddenly and dramatically, everything changed. One day Saunière was carrying out repairs in the church when he found that an ancient carved column was hollow. Inside was a bundle of parchment! Copied on to the pages were passages in Latin from the Bible, but written in a curious way, with extra letters, strange gaps, and odd logos.

Saunière realized that the documents contained ciphered messages. He borrowed the train fare to Paris and consulted an expert. A week later he hurried home. But before leaving he bought a copy from the Louvre of a famous painting by a seventeenth-century artist, Nicholas Poussin, called 'Bergers d'Arcadie' (Shepherds of Arcady).

Once home Saunière began to spend huge sums of money, buying land, building himself a house and terraced garden, lavishly restoring the church, providing the villagers with piped water and a good modern road down to the valley below. It's reckoned that before his death he had spent about eight million pounds!

Believing that he must have been led to a treasure hoard, curious investigators have tried to follow in his footsteps, suggesting what it might have been.

Though Rennes-le-Château is now an isolated little village, it once formed part of a great city, called Aerada, a stronghold of the Visigoths. They were the fierce peoples who attacked ancient Rome in AD 410. As they plundered and destroyed, they seized the fabled treasures which the Romans themselves had looted in their conquest of Jerusalem.

All empires fall apart in time and by the eighth century the Visigoths were reduced to a small area of occupation – around Aerada. Could Saunière have found the lost treasure of Jerusalem?

There is a second possibility. An early French king, Dagobert II, murdered in 679, is also connected with the area. Both possible treasure sources receive support from the two parchments which remain (two others are said to

172

be held secretly somewhere).

Both have the word SION hidden in them – and Sion is a name for Jerusalem. One has a message formed by picking out all the letters which are slightly raised above the rest. It reads: A DAGOBERT II ET A SION EST CE TRESOR ET IL EST LA MORT ('This treasure belongs to Dagobert II and to Sion and he is dead there' – or perhaps, 'it is death').

Another cipher refers to the painter, Poussin. The picture of which Saunière bought a copy shows four figures grouped round a tomb, and though experts say that Poussin never went near Rennes-le-Château, there *is* such a tomb not far from it, set in landscape which closely resembles that of the painting.

Moreover, a letter written in 1656 to an official at the court of Louis XIV of France refers to information which Poussin possessed which 'even kings will have pains to draw from him' and which 'nobody else will ever rediscover'. Could this be a reference to treasure?

It's all very puzzling, particularly in that there seem to be a wealth of clues but no solution. Saunière himself acted strangely, in that he both provided and withheld clues.

In the churchyard he deliberately obliterated markings on some tombstones as if he didn't want anyone to read them. Yet in the decoration of the newly-restored church he appears to have provided pointers to his treasure.

As a simple example, there is a sculpture of Jesus offering welcome to all who will come to him. He stands on a hill in the landscape of Rennes-le-Château and its surroundings. Quite irrelevant to the Bible story there is at the foot of the hill a money-bag, bursting open and spilling its contents.

There are other riddling pictorial clues, but no one yet has been able to find any treasure. So many tried that Rennes-le-Château had to pass a law against digging in the village.

Is it possible that the clues have been red herrings? When asked about his wealth Saunière would only say that he'd been given it by unnamed rich people. Was it the truth? Could he have found, rather than real treasure, a secret so important that he was paid limitless sums to keep quiet about it? After all, if he'd found gold and jewels, how did he dispose of them? Who bought them, and where are they now?

Even at the time of his death in 1917 Saunière was planning more lavish expenditure. But if there is a treasure it seems likely that its whereabouts will remain hidden in the fog of clues and ciphers.

48

Poltergeists

Poltergeists, or 'noisy spirits' to translate the German word, are responsible for things that go bump in the night, for strange knockings and rappings, and for objects which whiz alarmingly round rooms and crash against walls or windows. No one can explain how the queer and violent events occur.

Poltergeists like to smash crockery, break glass and throw stones: the earliest recorded incident took place

in AD 530, when a church official in Ravenna in Italy complained that he was being attacked by showers of stones inside his house.

There are similar stories from all round the world this century – such as the 1979 incidents in Birmingham. Stones were being thrown nightly at the windows of a particular group of houses, and despite 3,500 hours of investigation, camping out in gardens and using infra-red night viewing equipment, police were never able to see who or what was responsible.

Poltergeist attacks are alarming, though people don't usually get hurt and they don't usually last more than a few weeks. However, poltergeists differ from ghosts in that ghosts stay put whereas poltergeists may move around.

Like Mary's little lamb, the 1960 poltergeist of Sauchie in Scotland followed eleven-year-old Virginia Campbell to school. The teacher got cross when empty desks started moving round of their own accord. Crying, Virginia told the teacher, 'Please, miss, I'm not trying.'

Virginia was miserably aware that somehow the queer goings-on were connected with her. When her family had moved from their farm in Ireland she had been sent temporarily to stay in Scotland with an uncle and she was not very happy.

Strange knockings began to occur in her bedroom and heavy furniture was seen to move, apparently of its own accord. A church minister was called and witnessed some of the incidents, recording that Virginia was quietly in bed at the time.

After a few weeks Virginia settled down in Scotland and as she did so the noises and furniture moving stopped too. According to one explanation of poltergeists, this wasn't a coincidence.

When people are angry they often express their rage by shouting, stamping, or even throwing things. But quiet people, like Virginia, can't do this. The anger boils away inside instead. It is suggested that poltergeist activity is a kind of release of that anger.

In some way not understood, it is thought that the anger may be transformed into energy which can actually move even heavy objects around. The people responsible, usually young ones, don't know that they're doing it and, like Virginia, are often as frightened by the violence as everybody else.

One of the best-known cases in Britain occurred in 1952 in Runcorn in Cheshire. Living at number one Byron Street were Stan Jones, his widowed daughter, and grandson, seventeen-year-old John Glynn. It was only in John's bedroom that anything strange happened. There were bangings and rattlings, furniture was shifted and over-turned, books were hurled across the room, and an alarm clock smashed against the wall.

News of the eerie events spread and many people came to the house to investigate. John would not sleep in his room alone and had a friend to stay with him, but the violence went on.

Watchers were convinced that neither of the boys was engaged in trickery. Once, while the two of them lay quietly tucked up in bed, a clergyman investigator sitting with them in the dark heard books which he'd put down being thrown, and then the rattle of a jigsaw. He switched on his torch and watched the jigsaw box 'travelling across the room, rising about seven feet in the air'.

Sceptics would say that he had been fooled by clever conjuring tricks. It is true that some poltergeist events have been proved to be hoaxes. In one house where it was claimed that a poltergeist was making life miserable a clergyman was startled to be struck by a stone appar-ently coming from nowhere.

But neighbours had noticed the eleven-year-old son picking up a stone in the garden. He then thrust his arm through the letter-box. The conclusion was obvious!

No doubt other frightening episodes are stage-managed and the hoaxers get away with it. But conjurors can't pull rabbits out of hats without years of practice, and it would need just as much practice to make a jigsaw or anything else fly across a room. Investigators would soon discover if strings or wires were attached.

Conjuring tricks or mind over matter? Or are there really malicious little spirits around, waiting like genii in bottles to be let out to wreak destruction all around?

49

The Riddles of Easter Island

Of all places in the world, none has more mysteries than lonely Easter Island lying in the middle of the Pacific, 3,200 miles from South America.

This small island was named in 1722 by its first European discoverers, Dutch sailors who chanced upon it on Easter Sunday. Their second surprise came when they got close enough to see that lining the cliffs, as if its guardians, were colossal statues, surrounded by people in apparent worship.

Another was to find the islanders apparently of mixed race, with skin colours ranging from fair to dark. Many had red hair coiled up in topknots. Some had earlobes studded with great discs – when these were removed they hitched the dangling lobes over their eartops!

The Dutchmen examined the strange statues, some nearly ten metres high. They had no legs, only bodies and huge heads with long ears and tightly pursed lips. Some were crowned with blocks of reddish stone, perhaps imitating the natives' own topknots. It seemed a marvel that men who had neither invented tools nor discovered the wheel, could have carved, transported and erected so many huge statues.

Fifty-two years later, the English Captain Cook also reached Easter Island, but he found that things had changed. The people, fewer in number, seemed pitifully poor. The statues had been overturned and were no longer reverenced. It seemed there must have been tribal warfare.

The history of Easter Island in the next century was sad. Slave-traders came from Peru and carried off large numbers of the population, most of whom died. Following them came missionaries, well-meaning, but wanting to make the remaining islanders forget their past ways and beliefs.

But in the twentieth century investigators have become fascinated with the riddles of Easter Island, and have tried to recapture that past and understand it.

Where, firstly, did the diverse-looking islanders come from? In their legends they speak of two arrivals, the first led by a chieftain, Hotu Matu'a, said to be descended from gods. But was he from the Polynesian islands scattered in the Pacific to the west or from South America to

179

the east? (A further idea, not popular with scientists, is that the first-comers were stranded aliens from another planet.)

Someone who has tried to answer Easter Island's questions is the Norwegian, Thor Heyerdahl. He is a man who likes to prove his point: in 1947 he sailed a balsa-wood raft, the *Kon-Tiki*, 5,000 miles from Peru to landfall in Polynesia to show that these islands could have been colonized from South America.

Heyerdahl believes that Easter Island's first peoples came likewise directly from South America, probably in boats made from reeds. Many archaeologists disagree though and think that all arrivals in Easter Island were from Polynesia.

Wherever they originated it's clear that unlike peoples anywhere else they were soon obsessively creating statue after statue, quarrying an extinct volcano for stone. Half-formed giants still lie in its walls, while the heads of others poke dramatically from the slopes below. Sharpened stones, the only sculpting tools used, lie scattered around.

Somehow or other the completed statues, known as *moai*, must have been lowered down the volcano's side to await transport along special 'image roads' to platforms, or *ahus*, on the coast. Some never made it: they lie along the way, but exactly why they were abandoned no one can be certain.

How the heavy monsters (up to fifty-nine tons) were moved is another mystery. Islanders say that legs or no legs they walked, so Heyerdahl tried to prove that the statues could be manoeuvred upright, using ropes to rock and edge them forward in the same way as we shift heavy furniture. But the sizes, distances, and ups and downs of the ground make others reject the idea.

No one doubts that the statues were actually raised on their platforms by slowly levering them up on growing piles of boulders. Once they were in position white coral eyes with darker inlay were placed in the empty eye-sockets: only then would they have 'come alive', with full spiritual power.

But what exactly did they mean to the early islanders? How were they worshipped? Why were they placed on the cliffs? Up to 1,000 can still be counted – why are there so many?

When these questions have been answered, the island has plenty more perplexing problems, including decipherment of its curious picture-writing on wooden tablets, called *rongo-rongo*.

Easter Island is a long way away, but if you want to see a statue there is a 2.5 metre one (of black basalt rather than the usual volcanic stone) in the Museum of Mankind in London. Each of the *moai* had a name, so you can go and say hello to Hoa haka nana ia. He will stare enigmatically back at you.

50

Are there Aliens in our Skies?

At last we come to the question of UFOs, Unidentified Flying Objects, frequently explained as alien spaceships, which have been zooming in and out of mysteries throughout this book. Are these strange objects in our skies really spaceships from other planets, or can they be explained naturally?

Nearly all UFO sightings turn out to be of identifiable objects, most being aircraft. People have also been fooled by shooting stars, the moon, the planet Venus, or orbiting satellites; by fireworks, kites or car lights. After swallowing a fungus which makes them glow in the dark, owls have been mistaken for spaceships too!

Yet, after all these sightings are eliminated, there remain many which cannot be easily accounted for.

A case which hit the headlines in 1988 involved the Knowles family of Perth, Australia. Mrs Knowles and her three sons were driving to Adelaide when at 4 a.m. they noticed a strange funnel of light on the road ahead. Then it seemed terrifyingly to be on top of them, sucking the car up off the road before dropping it down again. Black powder seeped inside and there was a queer smell.

In a state of shock they drove on to the nearest town and reported to the police. The police saw the dust and smelt the smell, and also noticed some small dents in the car's roof. A local truck driver confirmed that he had seen the light in the distance. This story was quickly taken up by some as proof of the presence of evil aliens.

But others, interested in a scientific explanation, have suggested that it and similar tales indicate that electrical forces in the atmosphere, as yet not understood, are causing both the lights and the physical damage.

A similar encounter occurred in Britain on 9 March 1977. Two shift-workers driving home in Nelson, Lancashire, saw a cigar-shaped object with beams of light come out of a cloud over a nearby hill and drop down towards them. As it advanced their car headlights failed and the engine died. They felt a terrible sensation of pressure and sickness, but until the UFO drifted away they could not restart the engine and escape.

If this is the effect a UFO has on a car, how much more serious it must be for a plane. The most sinister stories about UFOs involve planes which crash.

But if such tragedies result from the attraction which a powerful swirling electrical force feels for a metal object, we would not have to believe in malignant aliens: though if proved we might think twice about flying!

What can we make, though, of photos of solid-looking

'saucers'? (The term 'flying saucer' has been used since 1947 when an American pilot saw UFOs over the Cascade Mountains in Washington State, and described them as moving 'like saucers when skipped across water'.)

A lot of these have been proved to be fakes. One recently-published picture described the 'spacecraft' as 'looking much like a spinning-top' – and that, indeed, is just what it *did* look like. Not all photos are provable hoaxes though.

There are also many tales of actual encounters with extraterrestrials, and while some are clearly the work of cranks, others come from reliable witnesses who have nothing to gain by making something up.

PC Alan Godfrey of West Yorkshire is one such. In 1980 he watched as a glowing, spinning light bore down on his car. Then he blacked out. Afterwards he was persuaded to undergo hypnosis to find out 'what happened' in the period he couldn't remember. He told of being taken into a spacecraft and examined by robots controlled by a leader called 'Yosef'. However, he later admitted that UFO literature might have influenced him to imagine the abduction.

In fact, descriptions of 'extraterrestrials' vary so enormously that, unless we imagine a constant stream of visitors from many planets, it's hard to reconcile the differences.

But whether one or five metres high, with or without noses or fingers, green or bright pink, most 'aliens' seem to have glowing eyes or shining bodies. Could we still explain the encounters as bright electrical phenomena which, because of all the space publicity, are interpreted as living forms?

It is, after all, difficult to believe that creatures from other star systems would so apparently frequently set out for Planet Earth. Even travelling at the speed of light, aliens from a planet circling our nearest star neighbour would take more than four years to arrive. From further out in space journeys could take hundreds of years.

The sheer number of UFO reports makes an alien presence in our skies seem unlikely. But if you've seen one for yourself, you may disagree. In the end, as with most mysteries, you have to make up your own mind!

Early Times, the weekly national newspaper for children, is an Argus Newspapers Publication, based at South London Press Ltd, 2–4 Leigham Court Road, Streatham, London SW16 2PD. Annual subscription rates are: UK £25; Europe £40; all other countries £50, and the newspaper can be obtained from *Early Times* Subscriptions, Speedpak, FREEPOST, PO Box 561, Hemel Hempstead, Herts. HP3 8BR. Hotline: 0442–234303.

THE ALIENS ARE COMING
Phil Gates

The greenhouse effect is warming up the earth so that snowmen could become an endangered species. It also means you may have to eat more ice-cream to keep cool in summer. But worse, it may cause the spread of alien plants which will cause havoc in the countryside and could cause some native plants, which like a cool moist climate, to become extinct.

Find out for yourself, through the experiments and information in this original and entertaining book, just what is happening now and what is likely to happen in the future.

Become a scientist and help warn the world about the dangers ahead!

LAND AHOY! THE STORY OF CHRISTOPHER COLUMBUS
Scoular Anderson

The colour of the sea was probably the last thing that Christopher Columbus was thinking about when he set off, five hundred years ago, on one of the greatest voyages of discovery ever made. His journey was just as adventurous and just as important as the first space flight to the moon was this century. But Columbus set sail into the vast ocean not really knowing where he was going or, once he had got there, what he'd found!

Now you can be an explorer by reading this book and finding out just what an extraordinary man Columbus was – how he managed to travel the world and put America on the map for the first time.

THE PUFFIN BOOK OF HANDWRITING
Tom Gourdie

How to write well with everyday materials. Write an alphabet in a tree of hearts, fill in word puzzles, trace letters, draw line patterns, have fun and acquire an elegant style of handwriting. These exercises have been devised to help you learn how to write beautifully.

THE PUFFIN BOOK OF DANCE
Craig Dodd

From ballet to Broadway, this book is packed with fascinating information for all young dance fans. From the evolution of dance in all its forms to dance classes, schools and techniques, the life of professional dancers, how dances are made and much more besides, this book captures the glamour and excitement of this spectacular art form.

THE EARLY TIMES BOOK OF CROSSWORDS

There are TV and radio puzzles, Hallowe'en puzzles, skeleton puzzles, science puzzles as well as straightforward crossword puzzles to keep you going for hours, days, weeks, months – in fact, as long as your brain can stand it. Whether you're a beginner or an addict, this book of crosswords from the *Early Times* will make you think and keep you puzzling.